Law and Irresponsibility

Law is widely assumed to provide contemporary society with its most important means of organising responsibility. Across a broad range of areas of social life—from the activities of states and citizens, to work, business and private relationships—it is understood that legal regulation plays a crucial role in defining and limiting responsibilities. But *Law and Irresponsibility* pursues the opposite view: it explores how law organises irresponsibility.

With a particular focus on large-scale harms—including extensive human rights violations, forms of colonialism, and environmental or nuclear devastation—this book analyses the ways in which law legitimates human suffering by demonstrating how legal institutions operate as much to deflect responsibility for harms suffered as to acknowledge them. Drawing on a series of case studies, it shows not only how law facilitates the dispersal and disavowal of responsibility, but how it does so in consistent and patterned ways.

Irresponsibility is organised. And its organisation is traced here to the legal forms, and the social and political conditions, that sustain 'our' complicity in human suffering.

This innovative and interdisciplinary book provides a radical challenge to conventional thinking about law and legal institutions. It will be of considerable interest to those working in law, political and legal theory, sociology and moral philosophy.

Scott Veitch is Reader in Law at the University of Glasgow.

Law and Irresponsibility

On the legitimation of human suffering

Scott Veitch

Routledge·Cavendish
Taylor & Francis Group

a GlassHouse book

First published 2007
by Routledge-Cavendish
2 Park Square, Milton Park, Abingdon, Oxon OX14 4RN

Simultaneously published in the USA and Canada
by Routledge-Cavendish
270 Madison Ave, New York, NY 10016

A GlassHouse book
*Routledge-Cavendish is an imprint of the Taylor & Francis Group,
an informa business*

Transferred to Digital Printing 2010

© 2007 Veitch, Scott

Typeset in Times by
RefineCatch Limited, Bungay, Suffolk

British Library Cataloguing in Publication Data
A catalogue record for this book is available from the British Library

Library of Congress Cataloging-in-Publication Data
Veitch, Scott.
   Law and irresponsibility : on the legitimation of human suffering /
Scott Veitch. — 1st ed.
      p.   cm.
ISBN-13: 978–0–415–44250–3 (hardback)
ISBN-10: 0–415–44250–8 (hardback)
ISBN-13: 978–0–415–44251–0 (softback)
ISBN-10: 0–415–44251–6 (softback)
   1. Law—Moral and ethical aspects.   2. Responsibility.   3. Human
rights.   I. Title.
   K247.V45 2007
   340′.112—dc22

                                                    2007024472

ISBN10: 0–415–44251–6 (pbk)
ISBN13: 978–0–415–44251–0 (pbk)

ISBN10: 0–415–44250–8 (hbk)
ISBN13: 978–0–415–44250–3 (hbk)

eISBN10: 0–203–94039–3 (ebk)
eISBN13: 978–0–203–94039–6 (ebk)

The headlong stream is termed violent
But the river bed hemming it in is
Termed violent by no one

Brecht

Fiat justitia et pereat mundus
(Let justice be done though the world perish)

Ferdinand I

Contents

Acknowledgements

A number of people and institutions have made this work possible and I would like to record my gratitude to them. The School of Law at the University of Glasgow supported my sabbatical leave in order to allow this to be completed and I am grateful to Tom Mullen, the head of department, for making this possible. Part of the early research for this work was carried out at the University of Canterbury, Christchurch, and I would like to thank Scott Davidson and his colleagues for the supportive environment I enjoyed there. I am grateful to the Faculty of Law at the University of New South Wales, Sydney, for awarding me a research fellowship, and I would like to thank Adam Czarnota, Martin Krygier and their colleagues for their hospitality and insightful discussions. I was enormously fortunate to have had the opportunity to discuss some early drafts of this work at a dedicated meeting at the *Altonaer Stiftung für philosophische Grundlagenforschung* in Hamburg. I am grateful to Valerie Kerruish and Uwe Petersen for offering me that critical space, and to Valerie, Uwe, and Tarik Kochi and Stewart Motha for their encouraging suggestions. Colin Perrin at Glasshouse was a great help in getting this book going, and I am very grateful for his advice on this and much else. Parts of this work were given as invited seminars at the Law Schools of the following institutions, and I would like to record my thanks to those who organised them and contributed to the discussions: the universities of Aberdeen, Bristol, Edinburgh, the EUI, Glasgow, Kent, King's College London, Leicester and Melbourne.†

I have been most fortunate to have made or kept contact with a wide range of people who have contributed directly—and some possibly unknowingly— to this work as it developed and I would like to thank them all: Gavin Anderson; Sarah Armstrong; Zenon Bankowski; Carroll Clarkson; Francois du Bois; Louise du Toit; Robyn Eckersley; Heidi Grunebaum; Yazir Henry; Neil MacCormick; Bert van Roermund; Wojciech Sadurski; Andrew Schaap; Victor Tadros; Neil Walker; Irene Watson.

---

† Some parts of Chapter 4 were published in *Social and Legal Studies*, and I am grateful to Sage publishers for permission to use them.

For written comments on later drafts and a lot more besides, I thank my friends and colleagues here in the Law School at Glasgow: Lindsay Farmer; Adam Tomkins; Johan van der Walt; and also my brother, Kenny. Emilios Christodoulidis has listened to and read more variations of this book than anyone else, and he has been unfailingly interested and supportive throughout; I cannot thank him enough for all this and more.

Given the argument of this book, it is wrong to say that none of these people bear any responsibility for what is here—but it is not of a culpable kind.

The ongoing support of my parents was essential in completing this writing and I am very grateful to them. Zach, Leon and Corin put up with my absences, but they contributed a great deal in ways of which they are not aware.

Finally, Ally put more into this than anybody. She has been generous and tolerant in equal measure. She has been an inspiration. It is a pleasure to dedicate this book to her and to Dana Rinksi.

SV
Glasgow
May 2007

Introduction

It is commonly understood that in its focus on rights and obligations law is centrally concerned with organising responsibility. In defining how obligations are created—as in contract or property law—or imposed—as in tort, public or criminal law—law and legal institutions are usually seen as one of society's key modes of asserting and defining the scope and content of responsibilities.

This book takes the converse view: legal institutions are centrally involved in organising irresponsibility. Particularly with respect to the production of large-scale harms—including extensive human rights violations, forms of colonialism, or environmental or nuclear devastation—and in contrast to conventional understandings of responsibility in law, morality and politics, the book provides an analysis of the ways in which legal institutions—their practices, concepts and categories—operate to facilitate dispersals and disavowals of responsibility, and it shows how they do so in consistent and patterned ways. In assessing how this 'organised irresponsibility' operates and what its implications are for both legal analysis and society generally, a sustained engagement with law's methods, operation and consequences is required. At stake is nothing less than a re-evaluation of the role of modern law in the production and legitimation of human suffering.

Thus the purpose of this book is to try to expose, in some detail, how law's involvement works in this and what it entails. It outlines, and then fleshes out by way of a series of case studies, just how it is that conventional legal institutions and concepts are implicated in the production and legitimation of extensive human suffering. While acknowledging that law and legal institutions can, and do, hold actors responsible for harmful acts, the essence of the analysis here is to show how these same institutions can, and do, contribute to the organisation of irresponsibility that legitimates such suffering.

The first chapter serves, perhaps more than is normally the case, to introduce the general themes of the book as I have just identified them. As such, I will not say more to develop them directly here. But it may be helpful to provide a brief overview of how the chapters that follow will pursue the analysis and to give an initial sense of the kinds of material with which it will deal.

Chapter 1 opens with an asymmetry—between the production of suffering and responsibility for it—that appears to exist and operate always as an inverse proportion: the greater the suffering caused, the less responsibility can be established for it. There is a common temptation to understand extensive and human-produced suffering as an 'excess', that is, as an excessive depart-ure from the norm—in this instance, a departure from legal norms that would otherwise define and constrain responsibilities. But the argument introduced here suggests something more problematic: that, with respect to certain instances of mass suffering, what is often seen to be an excess has its basis in the 'normal', in legal norms themselves. And crucially, what makes such suffering appear legitimate is the fact that legal mechanisms work to disavow the very question of responsibility for it arising. This is the more profound sense of irresponsibility that the book will explore.

The key concern of this book is not with illegal activities that cause massive harms, but with legal ones. In order to give a sense of the immediacy of this problematic, a first example is introduced: the sanctions regime in Iraq during the 1990s. During this period, up to half a million innocent people died as a result of a United Nations-led sanctions programme. These actions and the deaths they caused were not 'extra-legal', but had their roots firmly in legality; their 'excess' was authorised by the normative ordering provided by inter-national law. How does law contribute to, or account for, such suffering? Through a consideration of the example, the chapter pursues, in a prelimin-ary manner, the possibility that legal norms are not only complicit in the production of suffering, but that they organise the more profound sense of irresponsibility that is to be examined. The chapter closes by introducing three overarching aspects of legality to which we will return later in the book: law's normative claim to correctness (law as right); law's force (the enforce-ability of legal standards); law's priority in normative social hierarchies. Together, these features establish the ability of law to operate as a key mode of organising responsibilities, but *simultaneously* allow for and legitimise the proliferation of their clandestine counterpart: irresponsibility. Chapter 1 argues that it is precisely this simultaneity that is central to understanding law's social role in normalising the production of suffering, in ways to be taken up more systematically in later chapters.

Chapter 2 takes up the questions of what we mean by 'responsibility' and 'irresponsibility'. It initially considers responsibility by pointing out some lineages of contemporary understandings of the term as it has been under-stood philosophically, which ordinarily involve some reference to notions of 'answerability' and 'culpability'. But it becomes clear that the problems asso-ciated with responsibility and irresponsibility are not most fruitfully thought through by reflecting on definitions or stipulations. Rather 'responsibility' needs to be understood as a term covering a range of different techniques and purposes, the appearance of which in different social institutions and locations is thus better thought of in the plural, as 'responsibility practices', to use Peter Cane's term (2002, p 4). Hence, at this point, a key methodological theme is engaged that has two vital implications. Firstly, the idea of responsibility must, as it will here, be understood in the context of social institutions—including those of politics, economy and law—the different logics and forces of which will tend to work against the notion of any singular or pure notion of responsibility that transcends any such contexts. As such, secondly, what responsibility in modern society means and entails becomes (in Zygmunt Bauman's terms) 'free-floating', available to be given content and form in enormously diverse ways across a range of social practices, but, in this respect, also left open, as Bauman (1989) says of morality generally, to being 'managed'.

Thus we come to the central observation that this chapter explores: it is precisely through a more thoroughly grounded sociological understanding of 'responsibility practices' that we can trace the emergence of all sorts of diversionary mechanisms and tactics, in institutions, concepts and social forms which work to facilitate the dispersals and disavowals of responsibility that together may be seen to constitute the practices of irresponsibility. The chapter, therefore, details how modern social conditions and structures— including basic features such as the division of labour, bureaucracy, social roles and forms of responsibility 'transference' across social systems, and forms of socialisation and 'individualisation'—combine to allow not only for irresponsibility to proliferate, but for that proliferation to be organised.

Again, examples concretise these observations, the first of which in this chapter concerns problems identifiable in countries having to 'deal with the past' of gross human rights violations. What have been marked out as transitional justice scenarios tend to show, with remarkable clarity, what are, in fact, more normal or routine problems with the social production of harms. With reference to South Africa, the difficulties associated with doing justice to its apartheid past—of establishing, for example, who was responsible for what, who the perpetrators were and of bringing them to account in any meaningful way—show how easy it is for responsibility to be avoided should those who might be thought most responsible for the commission and production of harm gain effective impunity. And yet, this chapter demonstrates, this is the normal condition of the socially organised production of suffering.

Given these observations, what is *specific* to law and legal institutions in the organisation of irresponsibility? Chapter 3 concentrates on exploring the central claim of the book, that one of the key modes of disaggregating responsibility for harms suffered lies in the ways in which law operates to fragment responsibilities through its modes of categorisation. This chapter therefore descends into the 'engine room' of legal concepts and categories to show how they drive the centrifugal forces that allow irresponsibility to be normalised. It delineates the various means by which legal regulation operates in this regard, including central features of legal organisation such as sovereignty and legal personality, as well as techniques of legal reasoning. Each one of these plays a crucial role in allowing harms to proliferate and, moreover, in legitimating these through making responsibility for these harms disappear. In this way, an account of the amnesiac capabilities of legal thought and practice in the legitimation of human suffering is developed.

Again, to investigate and instantiate this analysis, two examples are drawn on in some detail in the second and third parts of the chapter. The first concerns the ways in which responsibility for the continuing harms associated with colonialism are disavowed through the deployment of basic legal concepts and forms of legal reasoning. In this instance, I look at the ways in which the supposedly post-colonial modern law of Australia—a law committed to equality and human rights, and set within a democratic political framework—can be understood to perpetuate the ongoing suffering of colonialism, while at the same time erasing responsibility for it. I consider this in the dual contexts of Aboriginal native title law and of legal responses to the 'Stolen Generation' enquiries of the 1990s.

The third part of Chapter 3 moves to the global level to show the enormously high stakes involved in law's role in the production and legitimation of suffering. Here, the ultimate test case for the thesis of law's role in organising irresponsibility is explored through an analysis of the legality of nuclear weapons and the consequent possibility of humanicide—of nuclear holocaust. While this shares some common concerns with questions of environmental devastation more generally, it is the deliberate and extensive planning behind, and the legalised organisation of, the possibility of global disaster that is most pressingly featured here. An examination of the International Court of Justice's opinion in the *Legality of Nuclear Weapons* case of 1996 brings the insights of the previous chapters to bear on how legal concepts and institutions are able to imagine the regulation of the use of nuclear weapons, despite the acknowledged horrific impact that such weapons would have.

Of all of the subjects of disavowal and disaggregation of responsibility discussed thus far, these cases best exemplify the macabre logic that is law's involvement in organised irresponsibility. Set within a broader trajectory of modern legality and its relation to social, political and technological developments, these ultimately apocalyptic possibilities have a direct relationship with the role of law and legal institutions in effecting what might, in fact, turn out to be the very *consummation* of modern law's destructive capabilities on a global scale.

In sum, Chapter 3 identifies the categorical ensemble of legal modernity's achievements, as playing out in any number of instances, to establish the impunities that constitute organised irresponsibility.

What do these insights suggest about the role of citizens and their complicity in these practices? The final chapter explores this question. In order to do so, it is vital to see how social structures and their interrelation currently overdetermine moral and political responsibility, and all too easily turn each into its other. Even in a non-apathetic polity—even in a polity within which human rights flourish—contemporary law's right, force and social priority, when combined in specific ways with other key social institutions (particularly those of the economy), organise *citizens'* irresponsibility in ways that it is extremely difficult to challenge. Chapter 4 excavates the conceptual and institutional lineages and practices that work on citizens to neutralise protest and to still unease. It explores how legal categories and institutions are complicit in letting 'us' 'innocent' civilians off the hook of responsibility for immense and enduring acts of violence perpetrated by 'our' governments. At one level, it thematises the relationship between state and citizenship, and the asymmetry of that relationship that can be identified through the analysis of legal categories; at another level, it engages a theme of social complexity, and how that works for both complicity and its denial, through a diverse range of mechanisms that leave no one responsible for state violence.

This chapter—like the book as a whole—does not offer any simple blueprints for overcoming these amnesias and inertias. Rather, it charts the terrain on which citizens' actions and understandings, and the limitations that they encounter, currently takes place. In doing so—and in line with the general thesis of the book—it therefore pays particularly critical attention to the structures, and strictures, that any forms of reliance on law for political transformation necessarily come up against.

Towards the end of her reflections on the trial of Adolf Eichmann in 1961 for, among other things, war crimes, crimes against humanity and crimes against the Jewish people, Hannah Arendt (1977, p 276) concluded that the most dreadful realisation that had come to her about the accused during the course of the hearings was, as she had put it, that he was 'terribly and terrifyingly normal'.

This book, in its small way, attempts to follow Arendt's insight, by describing what is 'terribly and terrifyingly normal' about modern law's capabilities in the commission and legitimation of human suffering.

Chapter 1

The disavowals of legality

The measure of human suffering

It is one of the defining characteristics of our time that humanly produced suffering vastly exceeds the ability or readiness to establish responsibility for it. Between the harms suffered—and especially in respect of suffering on a massive scale—and a finding of responsibility for it lie all sorts of diversionary mechanisms and tactics—in concepts and social practices—that work to make a connection between the two appear difficult, impossible or even nonsensical to establish. In all of this, the *asymmetry* between suffering and responsibility for its production has become entrenched, it has become routinised and so expected.

It is part of the analysis offered in this book to look into the nature of this asymmetry and to give consideration to the ways in which these diversionary practices operate. In particular, however (and this will be its key focus), it will evaluate the role of legal mechanisms—legal concepts and institutions—in normalising this asymmetry. The thesis here is that legal mechanisms operate as much to deflect responsibility for harms suffered as they do to instantiate it. It will suggest that, in many instances, legal mechanisms in fact play a key role in organising *irresponsibility* and that they do this as much as they determine responsibility. Indeed, part of the analysis will involve assessing how legal—but also influential moral and political—determinations of responsibility themselves play their part in assisting the proliferation of irresponsibility.

This interpretation goes against the grain of a widespread sensibility that understands law's role to be one that is focally involved with organising the responsibilities of legal persons. Across the widespread reach of its doctrinal areas and in its fundamental principles of attribution, interpretation and legal reasoning, it is assumed that legal regulation provides perhaps *the* most prominent, or at least socially effective, way of instantiating norms of responsibility. No doubt this sensibility is understandable, particularly in the context of an increasingly juridified society, but it is far from the whole story. In fact, that this sensibility has become a commonplace refrain for lawyers, legal interpreters and social commentators alike, while the production of suffering continues apace, itself stands in need of some closer investigation.

But let us return for a moment to our opening asymmetry, because there is immediately another reading of it that comes to mind. Perhaps most obviously exemplified in the atrocities that marked out the twentieth century as the most violent in all human history, that reading is this: how *could* responsibility be measured against the extent of suffering caused by human actions that resulted in over 100 million deaths over the course of that century's political programmes and conflicts? How could one begin to account for the suffering of large-scale violence in such a way that would make allocations of responsibility meaningful? What, in fact, could it *mean* to say that the millions and millions of deaths—usually, and increasingly, experienced by innocents and those already most vulnerable: women, the old and the young—could be made sense of and so be measured against a standard of responsibility? Is there not possibly something disturbing in the thought that there *could* be some symmetry here, some equivalence in thought or practice, that would provide the measure for understanding and responding to it?

The horrors of the twentieth century and the difficulty in attempting to understand them are marked symptomatically by the limits of language in comprehending the scale and nature of suffering. This limit is one with which we have become familiarised through phrases commonly found in that century's literature: the 'untold' suffering; the 'unspeakable' truths; the 'unimaginable' horrors. These and many other similar expressions together bear witness to the failure of language and imagination to come to terms with the extensive experience of suffering. And that failure of language is replicated in the realm of normative response; it is, in fact, bound up with it. 'Our moral discourse' writes Carlos Nino (1996, p viii), 'appears to reach its limit when dealing with deeds of this type.'

And this is partly what explains the sense of difficulty in establishing some measure or equivalence necessary to 'do justice' to these experiences and the limits they express. The asymmetry between suffering and responsibility for suffering finds its practical and institutional signification in the overwhelming fact that, again according to Nino's observation (1996, p 3), 'Silence and impunity have been the norm rather than the exception'. The sense of common measure—the sense of balance or proportion that underpins the Western tradition's concept of justice and which, in turn, informs the terms on which attributions of responsibility are commonly justified—here seems hugely inadequate in the face of such violence and suffering. Somehow, trying to grapple with and give *measure* to the horrors seems to do them an injustice: what balances *could* be made that would be proportionate to 'untold' suffering? If such extensive violence seems to disrupt the categories of our understanding and hence of our available normative responses to them, it is perhaps not surprising that silence has been such a common response.

But silence is inadequate in its own way. Silence operates as one of the crucial ways of *covering up* suffering and responsibility for it as much as it does to bear witness to these. Silence can mean different things: where it means impunity, then it arguably constitutes a second injustice, one that consists of the *refusal* to listen and respond to—to try come to terms with—that which cannot be told. The difficulty or inability to instantiate a just measure that would go some way to coming to terms with the experience of suffering does not mean that impunity is appropriate: the fact that measuring is difficult does not mean that it should be eschewed.

Observing this difficulty perhaps helps to explain efforts to re-imagine and rearrange institutionalised responses to massive harms in practical ways. In other words, these abstract formulations about limits may go some way to explaining the rise of 'quasi-legal' institutions and, in particular, the truth and reconciliation commissions that have flourished at the turn of the century. Under sociological conditions in which there is, on the one hand, a recognition of the limits of justice as proportionality, and a confirmation of the inadequacy, selectiveness and hence potential arbitrariness of any standard legal institutional response, and on the other, a desire to invoke principles of universal human rights, then alternative means of coming to terms with massive human rights violations have been called upon to provide a 'third way' between justice and impunity (see Du Bois, 2001). In this scenario, calls for truth, reconciliation, apology, forgiveness and so on begin to proliferate. As Derrida (2001, p 33) argues in respect of forgiveness, when, in the twentieth century, 'monstrous crimes ... crimes at once cruel and massive, seem to escape, or because one has sought to make them escape, in their very excess, from the measure of any human justice, then well, the call to forgiveness finds itself (by the unforgivable itself!) reactivated, remotivated, accelerated'.

But is there more to this 'excess' than mere immeasurability? Or to put it differently, might there not be other factors that underlie the treatment of these problems of immeasurability *as* an excess? Is there not a suspicion that we need to explore more fully just what might lurk behind the assertion that the asymmetry is one that pushes beyond the boundaries, beyond the reach of, standards of justice and responsibility?

I suggest that there is, and this is something that returns us to our central thesis, because perhaps one of the greatest difficulties in coming to terms with extensive suffering is that it was (and is) often the result not of illegalities—*pace* Derrida they were *not* simply crimes—but rather took place under the auspices of *legal* organisation. Legal institutions and legal reason were, in other words, often *complicit* in the commission of mass suffering. Writing of responses to the legacy of apartheid in South Africa, the problem here is one that Mamdani (2000) identifies as follows:

> One needs to recall the question Hannah Arendt posed in relation to another crime against humanity, the Holocaust: What happens when the crime is legal, when criminals can enthusiastically enforce the law?
>
> (Mamdami, 2000, p 60)

Here is the clue to what we need to pursue in more detail: the role of law and legal mechanisms in the production of suffering, and the role of legality in enforcing and legitimating this. When we appreciate this dimension, we see that the problem identified earlier as an *excess* and which we saw as tied to the problem of the immeasurable takes a different twist: the excess is not beyond law, but has its roots *within* law; what is *deemed* immeasurable has its roots within the measurable. The difficulty we identified a moment ago for normativity in responding (morally or legally) is traceable *back to* a form of legal normativity itself.

It is this fundamental problematic that I seek to explore. I suggest that not only is it a deeply troubling one, but it is one that, unless engaged with more fully, will continue to allow the delivery and proliferation of suffering that has gone on—and that goes on right now—in a legalised manner.

This may sound like an extravagant claim. Of course, we would not be surprised to think of barbarous policies as at the root of the problems of twentieth-century mass violence—but legality itself? So let me be clear about what I will not be arguing. I will not be arguing that legality uniformly delivers, in a causal manner, massive harms. I will not be arguing that law and legal institutions are incapable of holding people and institutions responsible. Rather, I will be exploring the ways in which legality *can and does* allow the production of suffering, and what this requires and what it entails. I will analyse examples where those with good intentions knowingly promote and have enforced legal rules that they know actually do cause, or will likely cause, extensive and unnecessary suffering to individuals (including the deaths of hundreds of thousands of innocents)—examples that are not distant, but right here and now.

The situation of our task then is one that calls for a dual sensitivity to an awareness of the proper limits in the analysis, but at the same time to an ongoing acknowledgement of the uncomfortable facts with which we are—or will be in the coming pages—confronted and which engender, or ought to engender, a restless engagement with the reality of ongoing suffering. On the one hand, then, to place at the door of legal institutions and concepts responsibility for any, or all, large-scale humanly produced suffering would be to give a false account of the historical reality. To repeat, it would be inadequate to fail to acknowledge the capacity of law to hold to account, either in fact or potentially, actors involved in the production of suffering. But it would just as equally be mistaken to allow belief in that fact to exclude, whether categorically, negligently or by inclination, from judgment and analysis the reality that law does—in the past, present and, if things continue in the same way, the future—also play a central role in the profoundly irresponsible production and legitimation of human suffering. A sensitivity towards the truth of the former observation should not therefore be allowed to constitute an article of faith that would magically redeem that of the latter.

It might be thought, then, that there is a profound ambivalence—indeed, almost a schizophrenia—about how law's capabilities are thought of and acted upon. At one extreme, let us imagine, there is a belief in the historical development of law as a progressive force for good, whether in promoting equality, fairness, welfare or whatever. At the other, there is—or ought to be—the realisation that the roots of modern law are planted firmly and inextricably in the ground of exploitation and imperialism (past or present). These roots have now developed to the point at which human, animal and plant life on the planet are jeopardised by a dominant way of life that is set in the context of legal norms according to which profoundly harmful activities take place, which are not illegal, but perfectly legal.

But the appropriate response to this perceived ambivalence is not to lose sight of either extremity: it is—and this is the more radical task of this book—to explore in nuanced ways precisely where and how the extremes meet. It is here that we must address how what might appear to be an excess can be, and often is, simultaneously rooted in the norm; we must examine why it is that certain acts are deemed by lawyers, politicians or moralists to *be* extreme—that is, not the norm—and so understood as a deviation from, rather than *as a part of*, the trajectory of modern law. In all of these variations, there are mechanisms at work in which legal and other means are deployed, more or less consciously, in enacting and legitimating disavowals and amnesias of responsibility, whether by dominant actors or interpreters. So our dual sensitivity should always remain in place and the notion of ambivalence explored productively, keeping in mind that any postulated schizophrenic characterisation should be thought of as RL Stevenson described his most famous character, Dr Jekyll and Mr Hyde: not as two different people, but as one and the same; to paraphrase Stevenson, even if it could rightly be said to be either, it was only because it was radically both.

Among the problems we must face up to, then, is that, not only does the asymmetry we identified register as an excess, but, on many occasions, it does not register at all. And so it will be necessary to inquire into why these examples I discuss so often do not present themselves as problems at all, as problems right here and right now. Prominent among the reasons for this is that the delivery of massive harms relies also on ordinary social processes—the division of labour, hierarchies, bureaucracies—within which legal institutions are set and on the capabilities of which they draw, the cumulative effect of which is often to splinter any coherent sense of congruity between acts and consequences. This is true both for institutions and prominent actors, but also in the—usually unarticulated—processes of defining what it means to be an actor, what it means to be acting and participating in the delivery of massive harms. As this takes us into some more familiar territory about the sociology of denial, it will also force us to think more clearly about the meaning of complicity. But again I will stress here the role of law in all of this, in a way that has often, it seems to me, to have been lacking in producing a more complete understanding.

So our key concern here is not with that which is illegal or criminal, but with that which is *legal*. It is with exposing and coming to terms with the fact that the cultural, conceptual and institutional crucible of legal organisation is able to carry out an alchemy that can turn mass tragedy into legitimate action, genocidal annihilation into the prerogative of sovereign right. So much more complicated and challenging it is, then, to see the task as coming to terms with the fact that the excesses are rooted in the normal.

That said, however, we should be wary of unexamined attributions of complexity. 'Complexity' shares its linguistic root with 'complicity' and in all of this we should not lose sight of the fact that, particularly from the point of view of the victims, the experience of suffering is not complex. 'Complexity' may make the asymmetry between suffering and responsibility for it *easier* to deal with for those who are not the victims, and so we should not shy away from considering law's role in obfuscating the effects of power in the structures of social relations.

Yet perhaps all of this should not surprise us so much. With characteristic insight, Rousseau (1973, p 184) observed that 'The strongest is never strong enough to be always the master, unless he transforms strength into right and obedience into duty' and it is with this insight in mind that we should approach our enquiry. Writing of the 'oppressive inequality' that can accompany the division of labour in society, where 'those who labour least get most', Rousseau's contemporary, Adam Smith, also understood this when he noted that what he called 'this enormous defalcation' is maintained 'either by violence or by the more orderly oppression of law' (Smith, 1978, pp 563–4). It is precisely this 'more orderly' form that stands in need of closer scrutiny, since the organisation of power in a legal manner relies on structural categories, modes of reasoning and institutions, part of the function of which is to provide a form of legitimation—internally and to the wider society—that presents itself as—that is, in fact—more than a straightforward exercise of strength.

'It is daunting to acknowledge . . .'

This last observation is central to the thesis developed here. Later in this chapter, I will make some final preliminary observations about law and will consider further the question of irresponsibility. But I want, in this section, to introduce an example that gives a sense of the stark immediacy of the kind of problems with which the rest of the book engages and through which the general thesis developed here may be begun to be explored. I said, at the start, that my concern was with the 'diversionary mechanisms and tactics' that allow for the asymmetries between harms suffered and responsibility for them to occur, and that my focus would be on the role of law in this. The following situation raises a great number of issues, not all of which will be dealt with here. But it engages our analysis by showing how, in a situation in which devastating effects were carried out under the authority of law, we find that knowledge of and responsibility for such suffering, fed through the prism of social and legal institutions, gets refracted into ungatherable parts. In the next few pages, I record what, in this instance, the suffering was, how knowledge about it was being made public, and what role law and legal institutions played. Some detail is necessary to appreciate the scale of the suffering.

From the time of the Gulf War in 1991 until May 2003, two governments in particular—the United Kingdom and the United States of America—enthusiastically and rigorously imposed sanctions on Iraq. Their actions were legal. They were given authorisation by resolutions of the United Nations Security Council. Both governments had direct and continuing knowledge of the disastrous human effects that sanctions were having. In 2000, John Pilger reported the following:

> In the [last] ten years . . . Iraq has continued to be the subject of sanctions that affect almost every aspect of life for the average Iraqi woman, man and child. With imports of food and medicine severely restricted, malnutrition and disease is now endemic in what was once one of the healthiest countries in the world. The latest UNICEF report says that more than half a million children have died as a direct result of sanctions. On average 200 Iraqi children are dying every day.
>
> (Pilger, 2000)

He reported also that two successive co-ordinators of the UN humanitarian programme in Iraq and others, including from the World Health Organisation, had resigned because, as they had stated publicly, they would not willingly take part in the human disaster they saw sanctions causing. Yet, Pilger concluded:

> US and UK politicians insist that the sanctions regime is necessary to contain the threat of Saddam Hussein. When asked on US television whether the death of 500,000 Iraqi children as a result of sanctions was justified [Secretary of State] Madelaine Albright replied: 'I think this is a very hard choice, but the price, we think the price is worth it.'
>
> (Pilger, 2000)

The sanctions were applied to a country that US and UK-led forces had just bombed to a massive extent in response to the Iraqi state's invasion of Kuwait. The first UN observer (Martii Ahtisaari, UN Under Secretary for Administration and Management) reported on 20 March 1991 as follows:

You asked me to travel, as a matter of urgency, to Iraq. It should be said at once that nothing we had seen or read had quite prepared us for this particular form of devastation which has now befallen the country . . . Most means of modern life have been destroyed . . . The authorities are as yet scarcely able to measure the dimensions of the calamity, much less to respond to its consequences. The recent conflict has wrought near apocalyptic results; Iraq has been relegated to the pre-industrial age . . . All electricity operated installations have ceased to function. Food cannot be preserved, water cannot be purified, sewage cannot be pumped away. Nine thousand homes are destroyed or damaged beyond repair. The flow of food through the private sector has been reduced to a trickle; many food prices are already beyond the purchasing power of most Iraqi families. The mission recommends that sanctions in respect of food supplies should be immediately removed. Drastic international measures are most urgent. The Iraqi people face further catastrophe, epidemic and famine, if massive life supporting needs are not met.

(Ahtisaari, 1991)

But sanctions were not removed and, throughout the 1990s and from this precarious starting point, the situation deteriorated. Despite a 1996 UN 'Oil-for-Food' Resolution, the state of health in Iraq remained desperate, particularly for those Iraqis already most vulnerable. A UNICEF Report from July 2001 stated that nutrition surveys 'show no improvement in the nutritional status of children since the introduction of the Oil for Food Programme in 1996. One in five children in the south and centre of Iraq remain so malnourished that they need special therapeutic feeding' (UNICEF, 2001). In fact, the Report continued, insufficient financial backing—less than half that required—by Western governments was 'seriously impacting UNICEF's ability to assist in implementing the Oil for Food Programme by supplying cash for transportation and installation of supplies, and training . . . The lack of funding for the nutrition sector is particularly alarming (87% requirements remain unfunded)'. Despite these funding shortfalls for humanitarian aid, the cost of the continued bombing of Iraq by US and UK military forces (which kept going intermittently throughout the period) amounted to tens of millions of pounds each year.

In its Report of 1999–2000, the UK Parliament's Select Committee on International Development had noted the following:

There is a clear consensus that the humanitarian and developmental situation in Iraq has deteriorated seriously since the imposition of comprehensive economic sanctions. Whilst details are often difficult to come by or to verify, even those who wish to maintain these sanctions accept that children, the ill, the vulnerable in Iraqi society are suffering. It is as obvious that Saddam Hussein and his ruling elite continue to enjoy a

privileged existence. Sanctions have clearly failed to hurt those responsible for past violations of international law. The deterioration of infra-
structure, the limited supply of food, the absence of drugs all affect the
poor to a disproportionate degree.

(2000, p 38)

The Parliamentary Report maintained that, while responsibility was in the
last instance that of the Iraqi regime:

This does not, however, entirely excuse the international community from
a part in the suffering of Iraqis. The reasons sanctions were imposed in
the first place were precisely the untrustworthiness of Saddam Hussein,
his well documented willingness to oppress his own people and neighbours, his contempt for humanitarian law. The international community
cannot condemn Saddam Hussein for such behaviour and then complain
that he is not allowing humanitarian exemptions to relieve suffering.
What else could be expected? A sanctions regime which relies on the good
faith of Saddam Hussein is fundamentally flawed.

(p 40)

It then concluded, on a more general note:

We find it difficult, however, to believe that there will be a case in the
future where the UN would be justified in imposing comprehensive economic sanctions on a country. In an increasingly interdependent world
such sanctions cause significant suffering. However carefully exemptions
are planned, the fact is that comprehensive economic sanctions only further concentrate power in the hands of the ruling elite. The UN will lose
credibility if it advocates the rights of the poor whilst at the same time
causing, if only indirectly, their further impoverishment.

(ibid)

In 2001, Dr W Kreisel, Executive Director of the World Health Organisation
Office in the European Union, confirmed the ongoing nature of the situation,
adding that 'about 800,000 children under 5 are chronically malnourished'
and concluding that 'unsafe drinking water, unhygienic environment and
poor sewage systems continue to endanger the health of large sections of the
Iraqi population' (WHO, 2001).

In a response to the mounting devastation, and under pressure from an
array of governmental and civil society organisations, attempts were made
during the summer of 2001 to alleviate the suffering by introducing UN
'smart sanctions'. As the UN Security Council Panel on Humanitarian Issues
(1999) had already made clear two years earlier:

Even if not all suffering in Iraq can be imputed to external factors, especially sanctions, the Iraqi people would not be undergoing such deprivations in the absence of the prolonged measures imposed by the Security Council and the effects of the war.

Eventually, a UN agreement on 'smart sanctions' was reached, which came into effect in May 2002. Most people familiar with the ongoing impact of the sanctions argued that not only was this measure obviously too late, but it remained far too little.

All sanctions were finally lifted in May 2003. By then, of course, it had been decided by the US and UK governments that sanctions were not working and another approach to the problems of containment of the regime (if not the suffering of the Iraqi people) had been deemed necessary. In February 2003, military forces of the US, Britain and Australia bombed the country again. Then they invaded. Four years later, another 100,000 civilians had been killed in the ensuing violence and, by 2006–07, two million Iraqis were displaced within the still foreign-occupied country and a further two million civilians had become refugees in neighbouring states.

There is little doubt that the human devastation caused by sanctions against Iraq is one of the greatest stains of our age. US and UK-sponsored sanctions were, for over ten years, directly involved in the deaths of hundreds of thousands of innocent people. As an editorial in *The Economist* had put it in April 2000:

> If, year in and year out, the UN were systematically killing Iraqi children by air strikes, Western governments would declare it intolerable, no matter how noble the intention. They should find their existing policy just as unacceptable. In democracies, the end does not justify the means.

This open challenge to the British government's policy provided a macabre echo of a reported conversation between Dennis Halliday, the first UN humanitarian co-ordinator to resign, and Iraqi trade union leaders who had asked him 'why the UN does not simply bomb the Iraqi people, and do it efficiently rather than extending sanctions which kill Iraqis incrementally over a long period' (quoted in Fisk, 2005, p 871).

Yet these actions, and these deaths, were carried out according to the law— a fact that cannot be emphasised enough. These actions were *legal*. From the perspective of legal analysis, then, we are not dealing with some criminal, extralegal activities. The consequences of the actions of sovereign states, under the authority of international law, as well as their key decision makers and representatives—prime ministers, cabinet ministers, presidents, etc.—were deemed to be shielded by UN Resolutions as determined by the members of the Security Council. In the 1990s in Iraq, doctrines of law, right and sovereignty put a veil over the killing of half a million innocents. Geoff Simons (1998) argued that, given the knowledge and persistent aims, policies and administrative practices (particularly of the US and UK governments), this amounted to genocide: 'In Iraq, we are contemporaries of genocide.' Dennis Halliday agreed, as did a number of other humanitarian observers. If this were the case (and it is a contested claim), it would confirm a variation of Leo Kuper's observation 'that the sovereign territorial state claims, as an integral part of its sovereignty, the right to commit genocide, or engage in genocidal massacres against people under its rule, and that the United Nations, for all practical purposes, defends this right' (quoted in Cohen, 2001, p 108).

If a fraction of such devastation were being caused by non-state actors, then it would be assumed that private, criminal or public law measures would plausibly be instigated to recognise and respond to the wrong: ordinary legal standards, such as reasonable foreseeability, recklessness or disproportionality of means to ends, would be invoked and tested by appropriate legal institutions. But, instead, under international law the state was able to *legitimise* the extensive and well-documented suffering in ways—including especially legal ways—that made the scenario appear qualitatively different from that of 'ordinary', private violence and suffering. State sovereignty was deployed as one of the most efficient resources for the production of suffering, yet there seemed (seems) to be nothing short of a deeply ingrained folk belief that the state's actions did not count in the same terms as the actions of individuals. In instances such as this, the 'law state' therefore plays a central part in the disaggregation of harms and causes, and its legal alchemy does the work of effecting impunity, of making impunity the norm.

What is the nature of this veil of ignorance that covers over the deaths of so many innocents, and for which law and legal mechanisms make up a significant part of the weave? We will return later to the more detailed aspects of the law of state sovereignty, but let us consider some final observations about the sanctions imposed on Iraq. Among the many things that are so striking about this case is that, all along, the information about the effects was publicly available knowledge, reported (if inadequately) in the press and academia, scrutinised by national and international governmental committees, and yet it failed to register in the public, political and moral consciousness in any meaningful way. (Arguably, it still does: there are no memorials to mark this brutality, at least in the West. Indeed, it is possible that the reader now is struck by disbelief: did it really happen; was it really that bad?) But perhaps this fact should not surprise us. In his analysis of the nature and origins of European imperialism, Sven Lindqvist (2002) concluded that:

> It is not knowledge that is lacking. The educated general public has always largely known what outrages have been committed and are being committed in the name of Progress, Civilisation, Socialism, Democracy, and the Market.
>
> (2002, p 171)

Yet if it still does surprise us, it does so most acutely because of the shock of a shadow of recognition, of something at once unthinkable and familiar.

It would come as no surprise to those who have felt the full force of Western law over the last few hundred years. As Robert Williams (1990) has written of the European conquest of North America and its effects on the indigenous population (although his claim is also a general one), this force was sustained by one overwhelming idea:

> ... the West's religion, civilization, and knowledge are superior to the religions, civilizations, and knowledge of non-Western peoples. This superiority, in turn, is the redemptive source of the West's presumed mandate to impose its vision of truth on non-Western peoples.
>
> (1990, p 6)

And within this redemptive fantasy, he writes—and here we find a continuity that stretches all the way forward to the devastation wreaked in Iraq by UN sanctions:

> ... the law, regarded by the West as its most respected and cherished instrument of civilisation, was also the West's most vital and effective instrument of empire during its genocidal conquest and colonization of the non-Western peoples ... a will to empire [that proceeded] most effectively under a rule of law.
>
> (1990, p 325)

If the imperial goal is different, the work of law remains. It should not surprise us, then—but still it does. This is, in part, because of an ongoing failure of sensitivity to the voices of those whose position is not our own, but who, in fact, know far more and far better than we do: the victims or their relatives. If we were to start our enquiries and our responses with the harms themselves and worked *back* the way—if we were to start with the bodies, the dead, scarred or emaciated bodies, the deadened, grieving or shattered lives, this one, and this one, and this one, each one—then, from this far more rarely adopted perspective, it would quickly become clear that the strands that might be thought to connect the harms suffered with some responsibility for them appear to have quickly become entangled, been broken, crumbled into dust. It is perhaps all too obvious, then, why this perspective is so rarely taken.

But if there is still some sense of vague recognition, even of this, then it nonetheless dawns slowly. Why? It is precisely because it proposes the actual as the unthinkable. Here is Samantha Power's experience of this, as recounted in her Pulitzer Prize-winning account of the USA's complicity in twentieth-century genocides:

Before I began exploring America's relationship with genocide, I used to refer to US policy toward Bosnia as a 'failure'. I have changed my mind. It is daunting to acknowledge, but this country's consistent policy of non-intervention in the face of genocide offers sad testimony not to a broken American political system but to one that is ruthlessly effective. The system, as it stands now, *is working*.

(Power, 2003, p xxi, emphasis in original)

This captures the essence of the matter at hand. It encapsulates the opening 'common sense' assumption that the normality is rational and reasonable, and that it is only deviation from it that constitutes a failure. But it also encapsulates the other, slower, realisation: that this failure is *not* in fact failure; rather it is, almost incomprehensibly, a success—because this is a political system *working*. And, as we have seen in the case of sanctions against Iraq, it can be a legal system working too. The incomprehension here is because we tend to be confronted by a kind of cognitive dissonance. (By using 'we', I refer to ourselves as background interpreters, as writers and readers; in the foreground, for the dead of Iraq, dissonance was not cognitive, but material, and frequently final.) The dissonance arises because we do not usually think of actions according to law as excessive, or extreme; rather it is rule-*breaking* behaviour that is usually characterised as excessive, illegitimate and irresponsible. It is part of the common understanding of law-governed behaviour that it is *normal* (both colloquially and in the sense of conforming to a norm or set of norms); such behaviour is based on pre-existing rules and principles, actions in accordance with which are legitimate and predictable, and generally characterisable as responsible. There is an assumption that law—particularly a law informed by, and committed to, standards of human rights applicable to everyone—is thereby a force for good. And yet in this instance (although it is not only in this instance), the law, our 'cherished instrument'—not simply the bad or misguided policy of reckless or self-seeking politicians—has been complicit in achieving the absolutely worst sorts of outcome. Here precisely, then, is a case of an 'excess'—the deaths of half a million innocents—carried out under the dark light of the law.

The question of responsibility

But what else are we to say about responsibility here: what sort of responsibility or irresponsibility is at work? We might begin by asking how those officials of the US and UK governments saw their own responsibility for the massive suffering sanctions caused. We have already heard from the US spokeswoman, Madelaine Albright: the price, she said, was worth it (even if that price was paid not by her government or people, but by those who could never bargain, including the hundreds of thousands of Iraqi children who would never live to know that they were Iraqis). In Britain, the typical answer was summarised by Peter Hain, the UK's Foreign Office Minister in 2001. He defended the validity of Britain's sanctions policy for reasons that included the following: 'Saddam Hussein's regime is a danger to its neighbours and to its people [and that] danger must be contained'; that 'Britain has a duty to play its role, as a supporter of the UN, as a defender of human rights and an opponent of aggression'; that 'sanctions were imposed to force Iraq to eliminate its weapons of mass destruction. The threat was real then. It remains real now. Iraq is still hiding weapons of mass destruction'; that 'Iraq retains a capacity to develop nuclear weapons' (Hain, 2001).

There was—to use Cohen's distinctions (2001)—no literal, or even interpretative, denial of the effects of sanctions. Albright's admission and the various and extensive official reports made these undeniable. Nor was there, unlike in Power's investigation into the US government's complicity in genocide through inaction, a question about whether these were actions that were positively harmful, even if indirectly. Rather, for the British government, such suffering was to be understood as attributable, really, to someone else. The buck stopped elsewhere: namely, with Saddam Hussein and his government. But the defence of this position involved more than this. In fact, so the argument went, the UK government was following an obligation—both of foreign policy *and* international law—in seeking to promote regional and international security and human rights. It is here that the legal institution plays a key role. On this view—and it is, as we will see in more detail later, a very Kantian formulation—conforming to an obligation made them responsible for their actions, but *not* for the outcomes of those actions. More specifically, following an obligation was the legally required, legally responsible, thing to do—'*Britain has a duty*', as Hain explained. On this view, moreover, if intervening factors stood in the way of the success of the policy—such as those attributed to the obstructions of the Iraqi government—then this could not make the law-abiding actors themselves responsible for the consequences of carrying out actions that were legally right. (As a consequence, as of January 2007, with Saddam Hussein and some of his government officials now judicially executed, the question of responsibility for sanctions would be entirely at an end.) Thus, the actions remained lawful despite causing extensive deaths, in the same way as the executioner who carries out a legally authorised execution is not legally responsible for the death that he causes.

So, in fact, the UK government was itself both responsible and not responsible: responsible for pursuing justified and legal policies; not responsible for the effects of these. What was deemed an excess—the legalised deaths of hundreds of thousands of Iraqis—was precisely, in this way, *normalised*.

Of course, this was also, to say the least, a very Orwellian formulation: the British government was responsible for the need to uphold human rights, even if this meant devastating the human rights of hundreds of thousands of those very innocents it was supposedly acting to protect. It was responsible for peace and security, even if this meant violence and insecurity. Given such contradictions, it is not surprising that many commentators have rejected as implausible both the arguments about international security, and the break in the causal chain between sanctions and suffering effected by the Iraqi government's obstructionism. On the first point, as Joy Gordon (2002) effectively argues, members of the UN Security Council, chief among them the USA and the UK, had being supplying arms to Iraq (including chemical weapons) to the tune of tens of billions of dollars during the course of the 1980s, so its threat to regional security was not something that could easily be regarded as being without international encouragement. As to the claim that it was the Iraqi government's responsibility rather than the imposition of sanctions themselves that was causing the deaths, Gordon argues that the most appropriate analogy here is with siege warfare, which 'has the effect of targeting women, children, infants, the elderly and the ill—those least able to defend themselves and those least responsible for the political and military policy' (Gordon, 2002, p 75). But to deny moral agency on behalf of the sanctioning powers themselves is, she argues, straightforwardly implausible because it suggests that *they* had no choice. It suggests, that is, that those who were maintaining the siege, with enormous and well-documented casualties, in fact had no control over their actions because they were being coerced into maintaining them *by* the Iraqi government.

Implausible as this sounds in argument, it was nonetheless the rationale for the operating policy. To put it differently, it was the intransigence of law *abidance* that, in reality, took on a feverish dynamic over the course of a dozen killing years, a force that had all of the relentlessness popularly attributed to the excesses of the revolution that devours its people by setting loose an unstoppable momentum. But, in this instance, it is the fanaticism of the norm—law-following in the name of peace and human rights—that turns into its other: an orderly attack on the possibility of human rights for those in whose very name it was carried out.

What marks this as a case of organised irresponsibility? To say that the sanctions regime imposed on Iraq was irresponsible could mean a number of things. It could mean that those who promoted the sanctions over time—the US and UK governments, and their officials—were able to use law to justify what turned out (at least in human terms) to be bad decisions. They could, that is, *justify* their decisions as a matter of law, as we have just seen, through the disassociation between the sanctions policy and the consequences, no matter how awful these consequences turned out to be. Irresponsibility, in this sense, would essentially mean a disregard for consequences in the name of upholding the law. But it might also mean something else. It might mean that these officials were able to rely on their legal obligation as a way of *evading* the very question of responsibility for their decisions and their consequences. The officials could, in effect, put themselves in a zone of *non-*responsibility, within which the matter of their responsibility did not arise at all. This would constitute a more profound negation of responsibility, in so far as it would not only put them outwith the range of responsibility for any consequences, but it would mean that both decision and consequences did not require any further justification (as good or bad), releasing the officials from any need to engage with, or be accountable to, critique.

If this were to be so, then it would be because the law would be functioning as a kind of amnesiac, a guarantor of total impunity in a very specific and powerful way, one in which law dominated entirely the terms on which responsibility could be made possible. Displaced onto the realm of impersonal legal regulation, no person or government would *be* responsible, the status of the sanctions' legality even dispensing with the need to claim that the policy was *justifiably* bad in terms of its outcomes. The question of *irresponsibility* would, accordingly, only arise as a function of perspective or standpoint: what would seem, from one perspective, to be profoundly irresponsible would, from another, not raise the question of responsibility at all. But from the perspective of those who suffered, this second reading would be *even more* irresponsible than the first, since it would make the very question of responsibility vanish entirely. And this is the crucial point, because here, in other words, the matter of legality itself would operate at once to put beyond measure the excesses of the consequences *and* make those excesses impossible to register in terms of *any* normative response.

This (as we might call it) categorical mode of disavowal operates as a form of preclusion that bars certain forms of experience and criticism from even being acknowledged. In this way, attempts to ascribe responsibility or irresponsibility do not even get off the ground. If we were, in this context, now to revisit questions of why these hundreds of thousands of deaths did not—do not—seem to register more widely as a matter of the utmost and pressing concern—Why is it still not recognised? Did not *enough* Iraqis die? Did they die the wrong way? Why did half a million fall short? *How many would have been too many?*—then it is the amnesiac reading of the power of legality that would ultimately provide the most decisive form of disavowal, since it makes not only answering these questions unnecessary, but it is unnecessary even to *ask* them.

This is however, to re-emphasise, from the victims' perspective, a most potent form of irresponsibility. It will not register their suffering adequately or engage with the assumption that actions that contribute to the massive suffering and deaths of innocents—in circumstances under which this is avoidable, when there is abundant knowledge of the effects over a long period of time, when there is intense pressure to alleviate their cause and the availability of alternative policy measures, and yet there is failure to act to stop the suffering—are, whatever else they might be, irresponsible.

To say that this was a case of *organised* irresponsibility—a phrase used by Mills (1956) and to be taken up more fully in a later chapter—involves making the following observations. The sanctions policy was highly regulated at various levels. Administratively, it took an enormous bureaucratic effort, from the drawing up of lists of what was not allowed to enter the country (lists that included obvious things, such as arms, but also an astonishing array of what was deemed to be 'dual use' materials, including medicines and vaccines), to the implementation of the sanctions, both internally and externally to Iraq, which involved constant and vigilant supervision of the programme. All of this required keeping in motion routinised administrative practices, because it was not possible to maintain a siege with the extensive consequences it had for twelve years without such organisation. At another level, it also took a great deal of political organisation, particularly in the sense of diplomatic activity, at the UN and beyond, as well as domestically, in an effort to maintain the sanctions in the face of official and unofficial counter-pressure. Finally, it took a tremendous amount of legal organisation. This involved, so to speak, a kind of dual use of its own: on the one hand, using the law to organise pragmatically the bureaucratic and administrative regime at its various levels; on the other, using the law as a legitimating tool to commission, sustain and validate the whole effort. It is in these senses, then, that sanctions against Iraq could be designated both organised and irresponsible.

To see this scenario as *exceptional* requires overlooking many of these observations. Moreover, to see them as a one-off—a sorry, single episode of regrettable losses, of tragic decisions having to be made in the circumstances of *Realpolitik* in foreign policy and international security from which lessons could be learned in the future—is implausible for other reasons too. Such a reading would also ignore the fact—or perhaps fit well with its denial—that the post-World War II historical context within which these events ought to be situated is not one of general peace punctuated by occasional mass killing. It is rather that of a trajectory of flagrant disregard for the welfare of those citizens who have encountered directly the interests and military of US or British governments, or their more or less covert complicity, whether in Indochina, Indonesia, or numerous countries in central and South America, with the millions of deaths that resulted in these places. That trajectory, writes Tully (2002, p 222), is one in which:

> . . . powerful states such as the United States and its allies profess support for democratic rights and the United Nations Universal Declaration of Human Rights while pursuing foreign policies that ignore, support or instigate their abuse and subvert international human rights institutions when it suits their economic and geopolitical interests.

The sanctions regime may not meet the criteria, as some have suggested, for genocide. But the fact that it does not is still telling for other reasons that form an important perspective on this trajectory. As Gordon (2002) points out, with reference to Vietnam and to sanctions against Iraq, even though the massive suffering was foreseeable and the consequences 'identical in nature and scope to the human damage done in "real" genocide . . . large scale killings directed at ethnic, racial, religious, or national groups *still* do not meet the requirement for genocidal intent, if the destruction is motivated by an economic or political interest, such that the protected group is unfortunately "in the way", is an unfortunate bystander that suffered collateral damage or has possession of wealth or natural resources that others desire' (2002, p 67–8, emphasis in original). It is, of course, clear that, in this historical context—unless it is denied or largely erased from public memory, which it so often is—mass violence is the *norm* not the exception.

Rather, what in fact *is* exceptional about this case is that the superpower and its allies carried through their actions with such conspicuous regard for legal validation—and that it 'worked'. This was not covert action, but successfully carried-through legal action. And it was also an action of profound and organised irresponsibility. At its most acute—in the form of the legal obliteration of responsibility for human suffering, as legalised impunity—it exemplified Harold Pinter's (2005) recent more general observation: 'It never happened. Nothing ever happened. Even while it was happening it wasn't happening.'

As a coda to these observations, although this time going beyond sanctions, the British Prime Minister was asked in 2006 about the consequences of the invasion: 'How do you sleep at night, knowing you've been responsible for the deaths of 100,000 Iraqis?' His response to this was: 'I think you'll find it's closer to 50,000' (Kampfner, 2006). There is a variety of more or less plausible interpretations that can be offered about the meaning of this statement, including some just canvassed in the text. (What did Tony Blair himself understand by it? I have no idea nor, I think, do I particularly want to know.) But it might show that, even when a link is established and responsibility attributable—even accepted—responsibility can somehow still mean nothing.

The juridical architecture

I will return to Iraq in the final chapter when I consider, in a slightly different context, the question of citizens' (especially in the form of taxpayers') complicity in the actions of their democratically elected government. But we conclude this chapter by outlining a preliminary understanding of law's capabilities in light of the foregoing. This analysis will be augmented in a later chapter, so here I offer three overarching aspects of legality that will be returned to later in the book. By introducing them now, we engage an initial sense of what law and legal institutions offer by way of being involved in legitimising the asymmetry between extensive suffering and findings of responsibility for it, based on some insights provided by the Iraq sanctions case.

What the 'juridical' form brings under contemporary social conditions are initially two features. These are summarised by Robert Alexy (2004, p 163) as 'coercion or force on the one hand, and correctness or rightness on the other'. Coercion, according to Alexy (ibid), is 'necessary if law is to be a social practice that fulfils its basic formal functions as defined by the values of legal certainty and efficiency as well as possible'. Coercion, in other words, is that which makes law socially efficacious. It does this by channelling force through the form of authorised legal institutions, thereby differentiating it from other forms of normative or physical coercion or social forces.

Law's claim to correctness is of a different nature; it is, says Alexy (1999, p 27), 'above all a claim to justice'. It is important to emphasise that this is a *claim*, as Alexy demonstrates by asking us to consider the following example. Imagine, he says (1999, p 28), a constitutional provision that states, '*X is a sovereign, federal and unjust Republic*'. There seems to be something intuitively wrong about such a provision, something more than it being just immoral or impolitic. Rather, that it is 'somehow crazy' signifies, says Alexy, the existence of a deeper assumption that is precisely law's claim to justice. The problem with such a provision is that it involves a 'performative contradiction':

> A contradiction comes about because a claim to correctness is necessarily bound up with the act of giving a constitution. This claim, implicit in the act of giving a constitution, contradicts the explicit content of the provision about injustice.
>
> (Alexy, 1999, p 28)

Thus a law that states its own injustice will appear as an absurdity; the *claim*, at least, is implicit that the law is just—it is correct or 'right', not wrong or unjust—and it is this claim, concludes Alexy, that 'determines the character of law. It excludes understanding law as a mere command of the powerful' (1999, pp 27–8).

If this can be observed in the realm of legislation, it is also true of the realm of application, as exemplified by the fact that it underpins, and is illuminated by, the traditional legal maxim (commonly employed by the courts) of *res judicata pro veritate accipitur*: as Salmond (1920, p 170) translates it, a 'legal presumption of the correctness of judicial decisions . . . That which has been delivered in judgment must be taken for established truth'. The nature of the status of this 'truth'—that it '*must be taken* for established truth'—captures precisely the nature of the claim to correctness: that it is a combination of the normative and the factual, according to which the legal norm's implicit claim to correctness stands *as* correct, and impacts as such on the wider normative and factual world. This is so even if, from competing perspectives, it may be claimed to result in a wrong or an injustice. Thus it is that the legislative or judicial pronouncement '*becomes the substitute* for the true and the just, *being held as true despite* its falsity and injustice' (Agamben, 2002, p 18, emphasis added). Agamben calls it a '*hybrid creature*' because 'it is impossible to say it is fact or rule'; nonetheless, its function and significance remain of undoubted effect—'once law has produced its *res judicata* it is impossible to go any further' (ibid).

The reason that these two aspects are so important to our study is precisely because, when I spoke earlier of the need to understand problems of excess or immeasurability *in relation* to normativity, we must now understand in this fuller sense that legal normativity brings with it a socially effective institutionalised force and the claim that this force is right or just (the claim to correctness). It is because of the former (socially efficacious coercion) that the latter (correctness) necessarily extends its reach beyond matters of mere internal legal validity and makes its claim to legitimacy effective in the terrain of social relations more generally. And it is this that constitutes the third feature of law in contemporary society: that is, given law's claim to correctness and its ability to enforce it, law attains a level of priority and prominence in social life and its normative hierarchies even when its effects may, in fact, be claimed to be unjust.

If we consider a further sociological dimension to this, then, where in contemporary society there exists an increase in formal law—that is, where, under conditions of *juridification*, there is an expansion into, and densification of, legal normativity within the fabric of social relations (Habermas, 1987)—then that double structure of coercion and right increasingly imbricates those social relations with the force and correctness of law.

A necessary effect of this is that, to an increasing degree, the juridical form permeates, structures and organises the available range of normative understandings, expectations and responses in the wider society. One consequence of this, as Habermas himself has observed in his later work (1996, p 460), is that it has come to be the case in modern society that law increasingly becomes 'the only medium in which it is possible reliably to establish morally obligated relationships of mutual respect even amongst strangers', with the result (directly pertinent to our study) that positive law '*relieves* the judging and acting person of the considerable cognitive, motivational and . . . organisational demands of a morality centred on the individual's conscience' (1996, p 452, emphasis in original). It is this result that sees law's measure increasingly predominate in matters concerning controversial aspects of morality and politics, including even the basic elements of the reproduction of social life—or their denial.

Given all of this, then, and returning to our opening asymmetry, we should understand that the reach and force of law's normativity is necessarily bound up with questions of responsibility and irresponsibility, even if we cannot yet say in advance that law is complicit with, rather than merely indifferent to, the production of suffering. That determination will depend on the particular subject under investigation, but where, as we have just seen, processes of juridification intensify, it is at least initially feasible to suggest that indifference is a less-and-less plausible understanding. As such, law's measure—its normative organising, force and claim to correctness—stands in a relation of *implication* to what is deemed immeasurable, including the commission of mass suffering and its normalisation. It is implicated in the 'cognitive dissonance' we identified earlier and thus in the very disavowals that establish impunity. And if this is the case, our task is to understand exactly the ways in which it occurs.

Chapter 2

Social structures and the dispersal of responsibilities

The mark of irresponsibility

It is something of an irony that irresponsibility grows historically with responsibility. On the one hand, the more that normative expectations—political, moral, 'humane', etc.—develop, the more particular practices that breach them stand out as irresponsible. On the other hand, however, according to the more acute reading of irresponsibility that we have just initiated, 'responsibility practices' (Cane, 2002) inadvertently bring with them practices of irresponsibility, the essence of which lies not in the breach of norms, but in the simultaneous removal of responsibility according to potentially complex, but nonetheless patterned, processes of disconnection, disaggregation and disavowal. Law and legal categories, I have been suggesting, have a distinctive contribution to make in these developments and our attention will turn directly to them later. But their role cannot be seen for what it is without understanding more fully the sociological conditions within which they operate. The purpose of this chapter is to highlight some of the most prominent aspects of these conditions.

We will begin to see now how central elements of contemporary social organisation organise irresponsibility. But it is worth emphasising that, in the specific sense to be developed here, irresponsibility should not be understood in some morally curmudgeonly sense—'That's irresponsible!'—but as the symptom, or perhaps even the encapsulation, of something more profound: irresponsibility is the mark of the obliteration of the possibility of responsibility. And our paradox is that it is in the organisation of responsibility that this achievement is made possible.

In order to show this, we need to look more broadly at the function of 'responsibility practices', their interrelation, and their underpinning in social structures and relations. It is important to understand that responsibility is not a single idea or practice, but a shifting notion, the characteristics of which are shaped by specific needs and conflicts, expectations and demands, and which, to some extent, also conversely influences the very factors that shape it. Thus, as an organising notion itself, responsibility plays both a weak and

strong role: weak in the sense that it is *susceptible*—susceptible to definition and redefinition in the logics and interests of institutional and informal
forms of power. Its strength is that, through these forms, it *can* organise social
norms in ways that allow disavowals and denials, and that, in doing so, it can,
and often does, successfully dominate alternative ways of thinking about
power or accountability. The reason why this dual aspect is important is
because, as we have already seen, when we consider from different perspectives the delivery and experience of harms and suffering, we see that different
forms of weakness and strength can co-exist, and that success and failure can
sometimes amount to the same thing.

It is, therefore, the deeper structuring of irresponsibility that is our concern
here. It is this that facilitates the impunities that have become the norm in the
asymmetry between harms and responsibility for them. In this chapter, then,
the issue is not whether we need more, or even less, responsibility for certain
things. It is not, in that particular sense, judgemental. Rather the issue is the
description of features of social institutions and relations that underpin the
impunities that will see practices, even systems, of responsibility able to
deliver devastating effects on human and environmental life.

Disappearing responsibility

Let me concretise some of these initial concerns by way of a rather striking
example. In the aftermath of large-scale violence and human rights violations, how are the harms that have been suffered—and that may continue to
be suffered—to be connected to responsibility for them? More precisely still,
we might want to ask, the responsibility for what, and of whom, *to* what or
whom? These are questions that appear, and are answerable, in different registers: as moral problematics; as matters of political principle; as matters of
policy options and choices; as matters for legal determination. In addition,
each of these registers may itself contain a number of more, or less, coherent
or competing considerations: some moral viewpoints may demand retribu-
tion for wrongs caused, while others will seek reconciliation; responsibility—
for example, in law—may be considered in criminal or civil law terms with all
of the differences that these two involve. Moreover, each register, each different to a degree, when considered more closely, necessarily intrigues with, or
rubs up against, the others: the moral with the legal, for example; the political
principle with the policy decision. The reason that this observation is significant is because the nature of any particular 'intrigue' may come at some cost:
according to one view, for example, the assumption of 'political or moral
responsibility without accepting the corresponding legal consequences has
been the arrogant prerogative of the powerful. Yet, in contemporary politics
the "contrite assumption of moral responsibilities is invoked at every occa-
sion as an exemption from the responsibilities demanded by law"' (Schaap,
2004, p 38, quoting Agamben).

In such situations, what is our *interest* in responsibility in the first place? Let us turn to our example. In the case of the post-apartheid transition in South Africa, in which a great deal of practical and scholarly attention has been paid to precisely these problems, there was a widespread assumption that determining responsibility was a prerequisite for the possibility of achieving reconciliation (see, e.g., South African TRC (1998) vol 1, ch 5, especially pp 131–4). People would have no need to reconcile with alleged wrongdoers who did not, in fact, commit the wrong: 'You've got the wrong man' plausibly negates any link of responsibility between the victim and that person, negates any *lis*, and hence talk of reconciliation between them would be out of place. Moreover, *acceptance*—not merely attribution—of responsibility would also seem to be a prerequisite for the possibility of reconciliation: one cannot be reconciled with the person who, despite a (let us assume, cast-iron) finding of his or her wrongdoing, still denies that he or she is in any way at fault for the wrong.

But in the transition to democracy and in the process of 'truth and reconciliation' in South Africa, what happened to responsibility for the wrongs committed under the apartheid order? Consider this claim:

> . . . the message of the 'reconciliation process' was that the perpetrators of state crime would be held neither accountable nor responsible, and their impunity was protected.
>
> (Pilger, 2006, p 227)

In one sense, this claim is wrong: the truth and reconciliation process offered by the South African Truth and Reconciliation Commission (TRC) *did* make findings of responsibility for the organisation of the regime and for the gross human rights violations committed or allowed by its agents. Many former security service and other state operatives came forward to seek—and many were granted—amnesty for the crimes to which they confessed having been involved in. In its reasonably nuanced approach, the TRC also attributed responsibility—of varying sorts—and blame for the functioning of apartheid across a range of actors and institutions.

And yet there is another sense in which the claim is correct, or at least encapsulates a sensibility that pervaded the whole process and its outcome: that those, primarily political and military, figures who had had most responsibility for apartheid, who had established and delivered its policies, who had been voted into positions of responsibility and accepted offices of state, who had together constituted the very political and military (as well as, to an extent, judicial) establishment, simply got away with it, retired to their comfortable and secure homes, retained their ill-gotten gains, or even picked up well-paid jobs in the new government.

How did this occur? Given the coherently organised force, the solid and expert brutality of the apartheid regime, we might think it remarkable how fragile and ethereal responsibility for the massive delivery or harms in fact turned out to be. It is remarkable how so many links in the chains of command—once, of necessity, carefully assembled and tightly secured—quickly broke apart, became unidentifiable, disappeared. It is remarkable how, with respect to responsibility, the constitutional order of apartheid—that is, the order constituted legally, but also politically, militarily and bureaucratically—was able to be *de-constituted* with all of the alacrity of a dropped bottle shattering into a thousand fragments. And like that, too, it is remarkable how responsibility then became impossible to piece together again in a way that would meaningfully establish a link between action and consequences *then* with consequences *now*. Many people, understandably, believed that responsibility in the case of findings of large-scale human rights violations would invoke consequences for the wrongdoer, most commonly censure or sanction; or, if the link between admitted responsibility and punishment was to be broken—as was the case with the amnesty process—even here, the provisions for granting amnesty still linked findings of responsibility with the need for the applicant to meet conditions, most crucially public truth-telling about their role in the perpetration of harms. Consequently, the effective impunity of so many key perpetrators, who were protected from *any* such consequences, was seen as entirely incommensurate with the devastating effects of their actions, a fact that for many people jeopardised the possibility of genuine reconciliation.

In its particular instantiation in the South African context, this problem seems to confirm the existence of something more commonplace. It is the observation with which we started in Chapter 1 that there is an asymmetry—between the production of suffering and establishing responsibility for it—that exists and works always as an inverse proportion: the greater the suffering caused, the less responsibility can be established for it. In this instance, it manifests itself because of a number of factors, one of the central problems being this: to have been effective, the force necessary to establish and sustain society-wide discriminatory practices and to inflict extensive human rights violations had to draw on a complex array of social practices, institutions and technologies in order to deliver its harms. None of these—structures it may be of government, bureaucracy, media, as well as of legal concepts and forms (including the state or corporate form)—is readily reducible to terms of individual responsibility, even though individuals play a role in its functioning. As such, this leads to two related dilemmas: firstly, seeking to establish the responsibility of individuals seems desirable (especially in the context of a goal such as reconciliation), but attempting this is to misunderstand the nature of how the suffering was produced; secondly, if attribution of responsibility for wrongs is to now-defunct collectives and organisational structures, this too seems inadequate to the extent that it fails to address the responsibility of those who made these very systems work at all and who are still around.

In this situation, then, it was all too easy for responsibilities to be dispersed and disavowed. In fact, the very attempt to fashion responsibility in a way that concentrated on individual responsibility itself contributed a mode of disavowal. Yet such organisational factors impact upon, even if they do not completely determine, the limitations on the possibilities for establishing responsibility and redressing suffering once the old regime has been overcome. The irony is, of course, that although the old regime is no more, *its* organisation—its political, bureaucratic and legal structures—seems to impact on current realities in the attribution or otherwise of responsibility. In a temporal sense, then, to paraphrase a famous jurist, the forms involved in the production of harms continue to *'rule us from the grave'*.

All of this seems fully borne out in the South African context. According to Mahmood Mamdani (2002), although the TRC stated that apartheid was a crime against humanity carried out against the vast majority of a population of over 40 million people, it recognised only *'20,000+ victims'* worthy of reparations:

> Could a 'crime against humanity' that involved a racial and ethnic cleansing of the bulk of its population have only 20,000+ victims?
>
> (Mamdani, 2002, p 35)

The apparent difficulties that the TRC had in meaningfully acknowledging these other many millions who suffered in so many similar and different ways at the hands of the apartheid system, and with this the failure to identify perpetrators adequately, led, argues Mamdani, to only one conclusion (2002, p 54): 'We thus have a crime against humanity without either victims or perpetrators.'

If this seems overstated, it is not by much. It was plainly obvious—in entirely different ways to both victims *and* perpetrators and beneficiaries—that, by and large, responsibility had, in fact, not only 'disappeared', but that, to use a phrase associated with authoritarian regimes, it had *been* disappeared. Through a combination of factors—but perhaps most of all through the sense that responsibility was able to *be* fragmented and disaggregated, not benignly or by chance, but in an active and organised manner—the asymmetry between the production of suffering and findings of responsibility for it had been sustained.

If the South African example is particularly vivid in this regard, then it is not exceptional. Undoubtedly, there are many features that are specific to the South African context, but many are not. The dilemmas to which we drew attention a moment ago are not only common to most transitional scenarios, but, more importantly for present purposes, they draw on conceptual, material and institutional forms and lineages that are common to all modern Westernised societies in respect of their economic, political, juridical, colonial and racialised structures. Indeed, if anything was exceptional about the South African case, it was the willingness to hold up to the light of critical scrutiny the workings of these very processes in ways that more 'settled' or non-transitional societies are often loathe to do, despite their involvement—historically and in the present—in the direct production of harms. But that even such an extensive effort was unable fully to grapple with these problems shows up, albeit unintentionally, the power of these very conventional and 'normal' processes in engendering impunities. If this extensive effort was not able to track responsibility in a situation as blatant as this—where the harms were so widespread, attested to and documented— what chance, we might wonder, would there be in less dramatic and more contested situations?

Thus we should not get too caught up in the in 'transitional' nature of this example. Although there were many brutalities specific to the apartheid order, the South African apartheid state sat within a common tradition of Western state practices and drew on many, if not all, of the resources of that heritage in establishing and sustaining deeply discriminatory practices. Besides, we might note, in a current era of Western states of emergency and emergency powers, of the reappearance of discourses around torture and 'rendition', and of racialised practices of security etc., all taking place in democratic states, the supposed 'exceptionality' of the authoritarian practices associated with the apartheid state inevitably seems less assured than it once was. But, perhaps most of all, it is from the vantage point of over a decade *after* the transitional period that we see not only how, as I have just outlined, there has been a genuine failure—or, from other perspectives, a success—to address properly the harms of the past, but also how the current inequalities, discriminations and suffering in South Africa are able to continue under a democratic, rights-driven and progressive constitutional order. If so, then we need to investigate further what I have called the normal functioning of social structures in the facilitation of the dispersal of responsibilities, because if the South African instance is striking, it is, as I have suggested, not unique. Taken together then, these are some of the factors that urge us towards the more general reflections to be taken up in this chapter: the social conditions for the ordinary production of massive suffering and why it is that responsibility for it can so easily be 'disappeared'.

According to a recent insightful overview of conceptions of, and debates about, responsibility, Christopher Kutz (2002) has noted that:

> . . . it is in understanding responsibility that we see ourselves as actors, creators, empathizers, and sufferers. It is in understanding responsibility, in short, that we know ourselves as persons.
>
> (Kutz, 2002, p 587)

If this is so, then it is necessary to ask just how it happens that the organised disappearance of responsibility—what I will refer to as the practices of irresponsibility—should be accommodated so readily within contemporary thought and its social formations, and, perhaps most important of all, what their active presence in practices of responsibility does, indeed, tell us about 'ourselves as persons'. In what follows, I will first briefly outline some observations on the notion and function of responsibility itself, and then, in the remainder of the chapter, consider in greater detail the social forms and expectations that are generally prevalent in Westernised societies, and on which the asymmetry between suffering and establishing responsibility for it rests.

The rise of responsibility

Despite—or is it not because of?—the difficulties surrounding responsibility, there is today, like no other previous time, a clamour for responsibility. In part, this is because the idea of responsibility has come, as Kutz (2002) suggests, to play a central role in how contemporary societies think about and organise their interpersonal relations. More and more, responsibilities, in a great variety of forms, are being demanded, both in the present and for the future, but also for the past as well. And it is significant, too, that, in tandem with the language of rights—rights being seen as a means to establish responsibilities—it is the language of responsibility that has gained such an ascendancy that one prominent commentator can say:

> The desire to understand the truth about responsibility grows, one assumes, out of a need or a desire to discover the meaning of life and what it means to be human.
>
> (Cane, 2002, p 283)

Yet for all such grandiose claims, we should remember that the concept of responsibility itself also has a history and that it is, in fact, a remarkably recent one. Here is a short account by way of a comparison (worth quoting in full because we will return to it again in this chapter), set out by Roberto Calasso (1994) in his book on Greek myth:

> The moderns are proud above all of their responsibility, but in being so they presume to respond with a voice that they are not even sure is theirs. The Homeric heroes knew nothing of that cumbersome word *responsibility*, nor would they have believed in it if they had. For them it was as if every crime were committed in a state of mental infirmity. But such infirmity meant that a god was present and at work. What we consider infirmity they saw as 'divine infatuation' . . . Thus a people obsessed with the idea of hubris were also a people who dismissed with the utmost skepticism an agent's claim to actually *do* anything. When we know for sure that a person is the agent of some action, then that agent is

mediocre; as soon as there is a hint of greatness, of whatever kind, be it shameful or virtuous, it is no longer that person acting. The agent sags and flops, like a medium when his voices desert him. For the Homeric heroes there was no guilty party, only guilt, immense guilt. That was the miasma that impregnated blood, dust, and tears. With an intuition the moderns jettisoned and have never recovered, the heroes did not distinguish the evil of the mind and the evil of the deed, murder and death.

(Calasso, 1994, pp 94–5)

It is, perhaps of all things, this last insight about modern responsibility that stands out: for the 'moderns', the distinction between mind and deed, or between intention and consequence, which finds its apogee in conceptions of autonomy and free will as the central understanding of responsibility, was to dominate the modern normative imagination. In the distinction between murder and death, we find, in miniature, one emblem of the disassociation of responsibility and suffering, and it is bound up with the emergence of the modern intention-directed subject. Responsibility, focally conceived of as individual responsibility, emerged as part of a long historical process, one that saw the rise of the autonomous 'individual' freed from the bonds of feudalism, fate and superstition as the primary locus of philosophical and political concern. Thus as Lacey (2001, p 251) helpfully summarises:

> ... most contemporary philosophical analyses of responsibility are grounded in notions of human agency which emerged in Europe in the philosophy of the Enlightenment. The idea of the self-determining moral agent, equipped with distinctive cognitive and volitional capacities of understanding and self-control, and of a universal human personhood underpinned by these features, have been of crucial importance to the gradual development of modern societies.

For the purposes of advancing our general thesis, it is necessary to spend a little time over the next few pages delving more deeply into some of these features, even if, for now, they may seem rather technical.

As a distinct term of enquiry, responsibility, in fact, emerges fully only post-Enlightenment—its presence is sparse even in the classic Enlightenment writers—and it comes to serve quite specific functions. At its heart, however, lay the notion of the autonomous individual, in theory equal (or equalised) with his or her others, and having the equal capacity for mental knowledge and will. As Nietzsche (1996) famously put it, 'the sovereign individual, the individual who resembles no one but himself . . . this liberated man' is taken to be perhaps the crowning achievement of modernity. And with it:

> The proud knowledge of this extraordinary privilege of *responsibility*, the consciousness of this rare freedom, this power over oneself and over

fate [that] has sunk down into his innermost depths and has become an instinct, a dominant instinct.

(Nietzsche, 1996, p 41, emphasis in original)

It is with this belief at its centre that the contemporary sensibilities of responsibility have become prominent and around which more and more activities have been brought within the ambit of 'responsibility', through its deployment in a wide variety of institutional settings.

This is not, of course, to say that modern notions of responsibility concern only individuals (as individual human beings), nor that individuals only have responsibilities that they can, or have, assumed or consented to; many responsibilities will be attributed and imposed. Nor will intention stand as the exclusive measure of responsibility, because standards of negligence and recklessness will endure. But these features will nonetheless, as Lacey (2001) suggested, be '*grounded*' in, modelled on, or devolve on the aspirational qualities of the autonomous individual and will be expressed through, or made compatible with, characteristics given to the individual as part of his or her '*rare freedom*'. It is, we might say, in theory at least, through the lens of the modern individual and his or her choices, attributes, worth and allegiances that responsibility will be brought into focus. The characteristics of this notion of the responsible subject are captured well by Ricoeur (2000, p 24) who, drawing on the juridical lineage, identifies three central and related ideas: '. . . that an infraction has been committed, that the author knows the rule, and finally that he is in control of his acts to the point of having been able to have acted differently.' The contrast with the Homeric heroes could not be clearer: as Ricoeur concisely expresses it, 'Fate implicates *no-one, responsibility someone*' (2000, p 26).

Hence we see the centrality of this figure of the individual in the modern normative imagination. Indeed, the fact that its '*privilege of responsibility*' has become, as Nietzsche (1996) suggested, an *instinct* shows up with remarkable clarity the powerful effects of this historical shift in modernity. And yet for all of this, we notice that there is a marked ambiguity already built into the core of these developments. It is signalled in the opening sentence of the quote from Calasso (1994): proud above all of their responsibility, the moderns '*presume to respond with a voice that they are not even sure is theirs*'. How could this be? Why might this 'sovereign' individual be subject to, or be the subject of, such radical *uncertainty* that it is not even sure whether it speaks with its own voice, in its own name? How can there be such an anxiety about its identity and its central attribute, responsibility? In order to try to understand these questions—because they will play a crucial role in excavating the presence of irresponsibilities—let us give some thought to how 'responsibility' functions today.

When there is thought to be some core meaning for responsibility, it is often taken to reside in some elementary, and etymologically-derived, notion of response or answerability: the ability to offer a response, say, or to face the demand for a response, and the understanding that that response may justifiably be met with consequences (such as praise, blame or sanction). As Norrie (1998, p 114) puts it, '"responsibility" involves both being "called to respond" (answerability) and being "found responsible" (culpability)'. But the fact that giving fuller delineation to any such abstract formulation is open to interpretative leeway and contestation as soon as it comes to giving it more by way of substantive content suggests that 'responsibility' eludes a simple or singular definition, and confirms the term's social and historical contingency.

In fact, given the amount of meanings and practices with which 'responsibility' has come to be associated, we get a better sense of its protean nature through paying attention to the diversity of meanings of the term. Consider, by way of example, an influential taxonomy offered by HLA Hart (1968), who identified four different forms of responsibility as prominent in contemporary discourse: '*role responsibility*', which refers to responsibilities and duties attaching to a particular status or office within an organisation; '*causal responsibility*', referring to consequences resultant on actions, but also on things or events; '*liability responsibility*' (which Hart treats as the primary sense of responsibility), which refers to the conditions according to which responses to a charge or accusation can be demanded and, if not justifiably rebutted, leave the agent liable to blame or punishment; '*capacity responsibility*', which refers to the competencies assumed or ascribed as conditions for responsibility (Hart, 1968, ch IX). Given these variations, it is necessary to understand that, as Cane (2002) observes:

> . . . the language of 'responsibility' does not mark a homogenous practice and concept best illuminated by context-indeterminate reflection, but rather that it marks a variegated and heterogeneous set of practices and concepts which can only be fully understood by context-determinate analyses.
>
> (Cane, 2002, p 25)

Responsibility today does not, then, mark a single notion, but rather a cluster of notions that exist as so many 'responsibility practices'.

Each of these, in its own way, involves particular forms and functions, the number and range of which goes far beyond Hart's taxonomy. So, for example, the following conceptions have emerged as candidates for thinking about and dealing with problems of responsibility (although even this list is far from exhaustive): retrospective and prospective responsibilities; act and outcome responsibilities; individual and collective responsibilities; human and corporate responsibilities; productive and preventative responsibilities; moral and legal responsibility; criminal, civil and political responsibilities; fault-based, vicarious or strict liability responsibilities; and so on, and so on (see, generally, Kutz, 2002; Cane, 2002; Bovens, 1998). Moreover, in addition to these varieties of responsibility, the interpretation of *each one* is taken to have to address, in its own way, basic questions relating to at least some of the following distinctive features: agency; identity; knowledge; freedom; foreseeability; power; capacity; causation; consequences. And even then, the *interpretations* of each of these in turn may, and often do, conflict, at their core, with each other or in terms of their application to whatever context is involved.

There are a few initial observations that are worth making about this. Firstly, it is important to recognise that 'responsibility' has not become fragmented—it was never a singular notion in the first place. Rather it exists in, or as, fragments, each with its own historical lineages and modern instantiations. The reason for this, however, is not because of any inherent conceptual ambiguities, but because responsibility—or, more precisely, responsibility practices—correspond to the complex terrain of social forces and conditions on which they operate. Such responsibility practices are situated on the terrain on which harms, benefits and solutions vie with a diverse range of interests, attributions and expectations. Secondly, this is not to say that certain interpretations have not achieved a certain priority over others. This is not, however, a result of the intrinsic worth of any particular interpretation, but a result of the ability to serve particular purposes or functions: for example, the dominance of individual, will-based responsibilities performs certain functions that foster a view of individualism that can be deployed in different ways in, say, criminal law or rational economic choice theory. Given this, and coming from a more sociological point of view, we can see that the role of 'responsibility', in its various incarnations, is an expression or symptom of the kind of requirements, interests, divisions and expectations that predominate in social orders. Hart's taxonomy therefore, perhaps unintentionally, provides us with an index of the roles that different versions of 'responsibility' play, and are required to play, in contemporary life. They do not tell us anything about the intrinsic nature of the concept itself independently of these roles or practices, because there is no such abstract meaning to be discerned in this way. Rather, it is precisely the variety of often competing forms of responsibility, and all of their attendant permutations and interpretations, that provide us with symbols *par excellence* of the nature of complex social forms, and the dynamics and conflicts they embody.

It is from this point of view, then, that we should best understand Lacey's important insight that 'ascriptions of and ideas about responsibility [perform] distinctive practical/normative roles in relation to various structural problems' (2001, p 254). For this reason, she argues, we should think of responsibility not as some timeless analytical concept, investigation into which will clarify its true nature, but instead as a *'normative device*—a matter of construction and ascription' (2001, p 275, emphasis added), which provides ways of dealing with and legitimating regulatory problems and solutions thrown up by modern social relations and their institutional settings.

To recall a question raised in passing earlier in this chapter—what is our *interest* in responsibility in the first place?—it may now be seen that the resources offered by these myriad forms of responsibility practices are best seen as providing organisational *capabilities*, fulfilling distinctive and varied regulative visions and requirements, which, together, Lacey (2001, p 275) identifies as 'technologies of responsibility'. Like all technologies, they are put to specific uses, they may be more or less adequate as such, and they will impact upon how a particular practice is itself understood and acted within. But, if this is true, then a couple of important consequences result, each of which may be perceived as potentially radical. What they suggest is that, under modern social conditions, we should be immediately suspicious of the notion that 'responsibility' has a prior or privileged existence independently of the social contexts within which it is found. That is, we must raise the question whether there is any independent, prior, reflective point of view that is not already complicit with the social conditions and systems within which thought about responsibility takes place.

This, then, leads to the first consequence: that, to the extent that the technologies of responsibility are the result—indeed, the very mechanisms—of social processes, then the idea that individual responsibility is, in some way, prior to, or separate from, the influences of these technologies is extremely difficult to sustain. There is, in other words, as Nietzsche (1996) hinted, something deeply suspect about that '*rare freedom*'—which, he says, the moderns commonly refer to as their conscience—because it has *become* an instinct only in so far as it emerges indissociably from the mediating, institutional and power formations of modernity. Such an 'instinct' is, in fact, the *product* rather than the *motor* of the technologies of responsibility practices. In much the same way as Hume (1978, pp 251–63) challenged us to see personal identity as an effect rather than a cause of understanding, so too individual responsibility—and indeed, as we will see, the individual itself—are the *deposits* of social forms, not their inaugurator. Thus any sense of their priority—of the priority of the individual and its responsibility—may, and may only be, a rationalisation. I will return to this point again shortly.

The second related consequence is more methodological. According to this, the tendency (normally unstated although assumed) to think that questions of responsibility might best be worked out in prior theoretical or abstract terms—philosophically, or as part of a moral philosophy, say— that can then be brought to bear, or shed light, on actually existing social practices becomes likewise less than plausible. If the different forms of responsibility are indeed symptoms of the needs and functions of social organisation, then it is unlikely that philosophical reflection on its definition will be very productive independently of an analysis of these organisational forms in their historical contexts (cf. Tadros, 2005, pp 4ff.). That is not to say that such reflection is entirely barren: it may offer some clarificatory insights, but most likely these will be of a type within which understanding of, indeed dependence on, dominant social forms is left unexamined. This is what Alasdair MacIntyre (1985, p 23) emphasises when he writes that 'a moral philosophy . . . characteristically presupposes a sociology'. According to this understanding, any morality will, to use a well-worn phrase, always already be situated within traditions of enquiry and analysis, and these are themselves inseparable from the social, the material and institutional, frameworks in which they exist.

This is a crucial observation because, at its core, what it notes is this: contrary to understandings that would treat moral responses or commitments (including those concerning responsibility) as, in a sense, primordial—that is, as indicative of, on the one hand, an awareness or responsiveness prior to intellectual theorising about such responses or commitments and, on the other, prior to, or at least separable from, social systems (such as law, politics or economics) that will come (or fail to come) to embody the claims of the moral realm—this understanding emphasises instead the impossibility of their separation. The reason it does so follows on from MacIntyre's initial claim, and involves seeing that there is a mutually constitutive relation between moral philosophies (and hence, by extension, moralities themselves) and the empirical conditions within which they exist, or which they seek to bring about. As he explains (1985, p 23): '. . . we have not yet fully understood the claims of any moral philosophy until we have spelled out what its social embodiment would be.' Indeed, he goes on (1985, p 72): '. . . it is not clear to me . . . how *any* adequate philosophical analysis in this area could escape also being a sociological hypothesis, and *vice versa.*'

If this is persuasive, and I believe that it is, then we should be very wary of any moral (or political) discourse that does not make every effort to ground itself in the sociological understandings of the conditions within which it is set. This may sound trite, but it means not only understanding the instantiations of any particular conceptual form—such as responsibility or obligation, or whatever—in the contexts of how they relate to the mundane level of policies, regulations or administrative practices, but also—and this is the key observation—that the presentation of, indeed their very *presentation as*, normative ideas (in morality or politics, say) must always be understood and placed in question as to their relation to, and implication in, actually existing social structures and their power dimensions. Why? Simply, because that—policies, concrete institutional and regulatory practices—is what these ideas and their presentation are bound up with, and that is what they are or will be—no matter how implicitly or deeply covered over—responding, or failing to respond, to or implicated in. There are no moral or political standards of responsibility that are not also implicated in their failure to be instantiated in actually existing practices. This is the more radical aspect and, if it is often difficult to see or glossed over, largely it is because the very conditions within which it occurs, that is, the highly mediated world in which the practices exist and operate, tend themselves all too easily to be assumed to be taken as given, and thus separable from the normative ideals themselves. But such an error, such a lack of reflexivity, will only ever provide convenient rationalisations and hence will always be potentially dangerous; dangerous again, that is, for those whose suffering does not register within dominant forms of responsibility practice.

Hence if responsibility is a 'normative device' and has been broadly conceived as, in some way, connecting answerability with agency, then the emergence of multiple responsibility practices signals not only an inseparable connection to power—for example, with answering to power or for power—but signals even more so that, with the deployment of 'responsibility', a part of its very meaning is that it is itself responding in its different instantiations to the various dynamics of power in complex societies. So if, as Hans Jonas (1984, p x) suggested, a theory of responsibility must have as its axiom 'that responsibility is a correlate of power and must be commensurate with the latter's scope and that of its exercise', then it is only by treating 'responsibility practices' as part of 'power practices' that we would be able to understand their actual roles for what they are.

And here, now, is the link with our general thesis. In order to understand the asymmetries between suffering and the ability to establish responsibility for it, we must understand how these very 'technologies of responsibility' themselves, as part of the broader social forms of power, also provide some of the major resources through which dispersals and disavowals of responsibility in society can occur. It is through analysing the complicitous relationship with these broader forms of power—in their diversions and distinctions, their priorities and interests—that we will come to a fuller understanding of the proliferation of irresponsibilities in the rise of responsibilities.

In order to develop these claims, we now need to pay some closer attention to the social structures implicated. As we will now see, it is in particular through the compartmentalisation, demarcation and limiting of responsibilities within, and selectively across, specific institutional settings that this proliferation can be sustained and, with it, the disappearances of responsibility legitimated. In order to show how this occurs, it is necessary to give more detail to the main features of modern social forms of organisation and their attendant mentalities. In the following three sections, then, I will highlight what I believe to be the central components of this: the division of labour and the significance of role responsibility; the meaning and effects of processes of individualisation; the transference of responsibilities through the distinctions and combinations of social systems, paying particular attention to the relation between the political and the economic. Even though I will do this at some length, what is covered is, of course, still necessarily selective. But each facet is chosen with a view to its relevance to the overall thesis and how it will allow us to put together a more complete picture of that which should not be lost sight of in all of this: the normal, the unexceptional, production and legitimation of extensive suffering under contemporary social, political and economic arrangements.

The division of labour and role responsibility

The first feature opens out from an earlier observation. When considering the 'disappearance' of responsibility, we noted how the difficulties or dilemmas of establishing responsibilities were partly a result of an asymmetry between how harms were caused and the difficulty of establishing the role of people in that. Oversimplified, the structure of the problem is something like this: the effects—wrongs, harms, suffering—are experienced by people; the cause of these is, at some point, human agency; between the harm and the human agency lie a whole series of forms and structures of action that simultaneously connect and disconnect the two.

Many, although certainly not all, of these structures involve elementary forms of complex societies that organise collective activities. These include, in the first instance, basic structures of the division of labour according to which individual activities contribute to processes that produce outcomes far greater than any individual effort. In the realm of production—as Adam Smith, an early investigator into this phenomenon showed—the organisation of individuals' work into increasingly specialised and compartmentalised activities allows far greater productivity than when the complete task of production is carried out by one person alone. This seems, of course, very obvious, because it is something on which contemporary society fundamentally relies not only for production, but also in processes of distribution, consumption, communication and exchange. It is so elementary, in fact, that its assumptions and effects can often be overlooked. Yet these early investigators, including Smith and, perhaps more prominently, Durkheim, saw that these processes and their effects had very significant evaluative and normative overtones in respect of social relations generally. Smith wrote memorably, for example, of the mindless idiocy to which workers could often be reduced by the repetitive nature of their productive tasks:

> His dexterity at his own particular trade seems, in this manner, to be acquired at the expense of his intellectual, social, and martial virtues. But in every improved and civilized society this is the state into which the labouring poor, that is, the great body of the people, must necessarily fall, unless government takes some pains to prevent it.
>
> (Smith, 1976, p 782)

Durkheim, in turn, realised that the general impact of the modern division of labour was, in fact, deeply paradoxical: on the one hand, there was an increasing individualisation and independence in modernity (associated broadly with the shift from mechanical to organic solidarity); on the other, an increasing reliance leading to an almost complete dependency upon others for even the most basic of human needs and activities. Hence the division of labour impacted upon the nature—and the very nature of the experience—

of community as such because, in so far as the tasks and responsibilities of labour were so divided, it allowed both for the unprecedented production of social goods, benefits and wealth, and all that came with those, but also for a (this time genuine) fragmentation of activities and their understanding from an objective point of view, as well as that of the actors themselves.

For present purposes, these observations have two centrally important aspects. The first is that there is an inverse relation between consequences—both beneficial and harmful—and the legitimate attributions of responsibility due to the compartmentalisation of labour as such. That is, the more extensive the division of labour becomes, the more responsibilities for the final outcomes are themselves disaggregated. Among other things, this aspect has come to be associated with what Weber (1978) described as modern 'rational' organisational forms, whether public or private, and especially with the *bureaucratic* mode of the division of labour that is so central to these. Where the division of labour can be seen as intensifying, it does so, so to speak, both horizontally (as in the image of the factory production line) and vertically (according to supervisory or authority distinctions). In this respect, compartmentalisation is achieved through the demarcation of specific tasks or of official jobs, requiring and producing in turn responsibilities attributed specifically to roles (this is what Hart's '*role responsibility*' is largely a symptom of).

We need to pay special attention to these role responsibilities, because they, and any sanctions attaching to them, are responsibilities and sanctions defined by reference to these tasks or jobs themselves, rather than by any other potential sources of responsibility, including those belonging to the person who occupies the role. As such, therefore, and as Weber (1978, p 975) pointed out with regard to bureaucratic organisation, it 'develops the more perfectly the more it is "dehumanized", the more completely it succeeds in eliminating from official business love, hatred, and all purely personal, irrational, and emotional elements which escape calculation'. Writ large then, official roles or tasks simultaneously connect responsibility with technical capability for a circumscribed range of activity—that is, they limit responsibility to roles—and thus disconnect alternative value bases of accountability or agency.

Where this is so, processes of rationalisation and compartmentalisation are therefore not limited to their positive benefits—such as calculability or efficiency in production—but also come to play a central role in segregating harms from responsibility. Sociologist Zygmunt Bauman (1989) takes up this observation in his highly regarded book investigating the connections between the ideas and processes of modernity and the Holocaust. In it, he also notes the dual potential of the division of labour, but concludes, in the following stark terms:

> . . . mediating the action, splitting the action between stages delineated and set apart by hierarchy of authority, and cutting the action across

through functional specialization is one of the most salient and proudly advertised achievements of our rational society . . . [Yet] immanently and irretrievably, the process of rationalization facilitates behaviour that is inhuman and cruel in its consequences, if not in its intentions. *The more rational is the organisation of action, the easier it is to cause suffering—* and remain at peace with itself.

(Bauman, 1989, p 155, emphasis in original)

It is worth paying particular attention to certain features of this description. We may note that, despite the purported rise of 'the individual' in the broad developments associated with modernity, we encounter again the ambiguity concerning it; in this instance, the individual becomes merely the *conduit* for larger processes and definitions *over which* he or she has little, or no, control. It is this that directly connects Weber's observation about the 'dehumanisation' effects of organisations and the 'inhuman' nature of the consequences that such processes can readily produce. As part of this, the *separation* between intention and consequence—reminiscent of Calasso's observation about distinguishing the mind and the deed—is firmly entrenched through a limitation of responsibility only to the defined task at hand. Thus a disaggregation is made possible and carried through by, among other things, severing the link between causes and outcomes (initial agents and ultimate victims of harm) that is, furthermore, (circularly) legitimated by setting individual wrongdoing as the measure of responsibility that, when not found, is sufficient to negate responsibility for ultimate consequences.

Another point to take from Bauman's observation is crucial: the designated *rationality* of these forms of organisation does not remain, symbolically at least, exclusively *within* the domain of the processes of compartmentalisation and the technical or instrumental capabilities associated with them; rather these forms contribute to a more socially widespread presumption of general rationality in their favour. This is what Bauman is getting at when he points out that the knowledge of suffering does not necessarily register *despite* the role of these rational processes in producing suffering as an overall effect of its organisational capabilities. Hence the 'rational' nature of the form of organisation performs a legitimation function that can have a broader amnesic—or as Bauman puts it, irenic—impact according to which harms may be perpetuated and disavowed, even as they are produced regularly and 'rationally'. This may be, in part, the result of the amnesic effects of the particular role-based actions themselves—a kind of parallel to the mindless idiocy of Smith's worker—the very repetition of which normalises and dulls input from any other critical source as to the overall nature of the enterprise. But far more importantly, it is the result of the fact that these consequences are given 'structural' encouragement and validation through promoting and maintaining the perception that rule following and role fulfilment, in the context of institutionally defined and bounded tasks within hierarchies of authority, are worthy activities *in themselves*. In addition, the division of labour into role responsibilities has the potential to reach right the way down to constitute the experience of the individual in that role and comes to instantiate their role-understanding *as* self-understanding. Fulfilment of role responsibilities—and these take place across a great range of discrete activities—comes to be seen, then, not as contributing a set of virtues that together make a good worker or citizen or whatever, but are increasingly defined as themselves fulfilling a role that does not engender the epithets of general excellence or virtue. In fact, they potentially come to embody something *radically different*: the precise opposite; namely, the transformation of role-responsibility into non-responsibility in the fulfilment of that role. That is, under the various roles that the individual occupies and over which he or she has little or no defining capacity, the actor's *lack* of responsibility applies not only to distant consequences, but *even to his or her own* actions in that role. Under such conditions, the actor, 'no longer sees himself as the efficient cause of *his own* actions', this having been subsumed under and attributed to the role itself (Milgram, 1974, p xii, emphasis added). But this 'agentic' state is, says Bauman (1989, p 162), 'the opposite of the state of autonomy'.

It is precisely this, these forms of organisation and their effects on individuals, that led Stanley Milgram (1974)—whose experiments did a great deal to expose the significance of the conditions and settings of compartmentalisation, authority and expertise on social action when it comes to obedience and the 'normal' production of harm—to describe the key consequence of such processes and the mindsets they engender in the following way:

> There is a fragmentation of the total human act; no one man decides to carry out the evil act and is confronted with its consequences. The person who assumes full responsibility for the act has evaporated.
>
> (Milgram, 1974, p 11)

This, he concludes, 'is the most common characteristic of socially organized evil in modern society'.

Let us, at this point, turn to the second general aspect associated with the division of labour. This relates to how these features of rationalisation and the division of labour further involve the creation and entrenchment of spatial and temporal *distances* between harm and responsibility for its production. Paradoxically, as Durkheim observed, increased interdependency—say, at the material level—also induces perceptions of increased isolation; while the division of labour, in one sense, provides an integrative mechanism in complex societies, it also brings with it the atomism associated with modern individualism. As part of this, not only are distances across space and time created, but conceptions of space and time are themselves constructed in ways that correspond to the patterns of the division of labour. And it is the *productive* nature of this that alerts us to the fact that dynamics of interest (if not intention) play a central role here. Thus, as regards distance, for example, although we hear a great deal about the contracting space of a globalised world (travel, integrated markets, speed of technological communiction, etc.), the experience of mass poverty is kept distant from the wealthy through these self-same structures, used as ways of maintaining barriers to comprehension or complicity. As Pablo Richard, the Chilean theologian, powerfully expressed it at the time of the fall of Berlin Wall, another wall, this time 'between the rich and poor is being built, so that poverty does not annoy the powerful and the poor are obliged to die in the silence of history' (quoted in Farmer, 2003, p 50). Likewise, with regard to the temporal dimension, the immediacy of suffering may be distanced by being highly mediated: somehow, the time of these harms is never now, *right now*. (Are they *really* happening right now?) To the extent that there is a simultaneity, it seems to happen in a parallel time, not 'our' time, or in 'our' place. To return to the case of sanctions against Iraq, when Tony Blair says in London that sanctions are to continue, he is not saying directly to this child, in this hospital room, at this time, *right here and right now*: 'I refuse to give you this drug that you need.' This may be the ultimate effect of his words, but they do not appear as this; somehow, the effects will happen some time, and will have happened somewhere, but from London, the drug is never retracted in its immediacy right here and right now, even though it is happening right *there* and right now.

We can see how this fits in well with the points made a moment ago about the disaggregations of responsibility. But let us just consider that last example a moment longer, because it may be thought that it is a naive one: of course, the two situations—being in the children's hospital ward and sitting in 10 Downing Street—are not the same. But this is precisely the point: its very awkwardness, the sense of its being overstated, demands and relies on all of the various mediating or building blocks to be established in order that this example does not seem to make sense. (As soon as we explore the question of why they are they not the same, we necessarily have to begin to list all of the intervening factors that go to build up these blockages, which are themselves the very structures we are concerned with. We must start, in other words, by detailing all of the complexities involved and, in this way, patiently explain our 'intuition' about the difference—to 'us' although not to 'them'—between murder and death.) The fact is, of course, that where the spatial and temporal separations and distances are treated as *objective*, as standing outside and above the particular activities going on within them, there is a failure to understand that their *appearance* as such (*as* objective) is not—cannot be—because they are the necessary or natural components that frame actions or their co-ordination. Such separations and distances do not happen within absolutely given space–time co-ordinates, because such co-ordinates, when it comes to *social* action, are always tied to a stake or perspective; and in turn, the temporal and spatial dimensions are involved in reacting to, or positioning, this stake or perspective. Hence these core spatial and temporal dimensions, so often assumed to be external and neutral (the passing of time, the distance of so many miles, etc.), are far from being such; on the contrary, as David Harvey points out (1989, p 204, emphasis added), '*objective* conceptions of time and space are necessarily *created through* material practices and processes which serve to reproduce social life'. Given this, the disaggregation of responsibilities into ungatherable parts has many dimensions, and they need to be understood in the context of institutions, material-conceptual practices, micro- and macro-locations across time and space, and in how they contribute to the dominant perceptions of these very space–time co-ordinates.

In this way, we come to understand how 'responsibility', under modern conditions of a thoroughgoing division of labour, has, in Bauman's terms, become 'free-floating' (1989, p 163), although we should take care to note that this does not mean responsibility 'floats freely' from its social locations. In fact, the opposite is true: it may be unanchored only in the sense of having no tie to some singular or prior notion of responsibility, but it is—in fact, because it is—firmly attached to the variety of socially available role formations. And in this we find further evidence of the simultaneous proliferation of responsibilities and all of the necessary elements for their disavowal. At its most extreme, it means that such forms of social organisation are, as Bauman puts it (ibid), 'as a whole . . . instrument[s] to obliterate responsibility'.

Drawing together the insights of his important analysis, Bauman concludes by identifying a number of features of contemporary Westernised societies in which morality is 'managed', which may stand as a summary of aspects of the foregoing:

> [The] social production of distance, which either annuls or weakens the pressure of moral responsibility; substitution of technical for moral responsibility, which effectively conceals the moral significance of the action; and the technology of segregation and separation, which promotes indifference to the plight of the Other which otherwise would be subject to moral evaluation and morally motivated response.
>
> (Bauman, 1989, p 199)

To this, he adds one final feature, one that will be important to our study, but which we will leave aside for now. That feature is, he says, 'that all these morality-eroding mechanisms are further strengthened by the principle of sovereignty of state powers usurping supreme ethical authority on behalf of societies they rule' (ibid).

Given these features, 'responsibility practices' can, as I have suggested, only properly be understood as being constitutively bound up with the 'power practices' of system-specific modes of organisation and expectations, and the divisions and demarcations they set in place. (In fact, for this very reason, I would dispute Bauman's sense of the priority of an '*Other-directed morality*', if for no other reason than that, if his sociological insights are indeed correct, then this pure notion of responsibility that remains untouched or primal and to which reference can be made seems implausible under these conditions.) It is in precisely this way that 'responsibility', to recall Lacey's terminology, is used as *'technology'*—a 'normative device'—in organising how role responsibilities are parcelled out, and in setting out the terms of their function and limits. We conclude this section, then, by making the following observations about what this 'technology' may be used to do.

Firstly, it attaches responsibilities within roles that define, more or less formally, the specific tasks of the job, office or status. In most cases, such responsibilities will tend to be, again more or less formally, established institutionally; that is, responsibilities will be attributed and given definition not by the agent themselves, but rather with reference to that part of the activity or process with, or within, which they are engaged. This extends all the way from the factory worker to the constitutionally prescribed offices of ministers of state. In this way, the obligations—and the fulfilment of the obligations—of the task, office or status are circumscribed accordingly. 'Acting responsibly' therefore means acting according to these obligations. When it comes to role responsibility then, responsible action means action within the permissible range, as established by the obligations of the role, making it irresponsible not so to act. Furthermore, failure to fulfil these obligations may lead to legitimate censure, but it will be censure *only* in accordance with that role. Beyond the defined role is a realm of *non*-responsibility. Like Portia's injunction to Shylock that he take only a pound of flesh, responsibility in this sense means no less *and* no more.

Here, then, is a key insight: breach of the responsibilities attached to the role will be irresponsible, but their fulfilment will not be. Role responsibility, in this sense, should also be seen to draw on a powerful and influential intellectual lineage in modernity, one that bolsters the belief that action according to a set rule or role is itself blameless. (I will return explicitly to this lineage with specific regard to legal roles and obligations in the next chapter.) But the reason that these abstract formulations and intellectual lineages are so significant is because of the way in which they have become so commonplace, as understandings and justifications of role-based action under modern social conditions. Thus they are, usually implicitly, of course, deployed successfully in all manner of very mundane and ordinary settings, and so have achieved enormously powerful legitimating force. The bureaucrat who is just doing his or her job; the professional fulfilling his or her role; the weapons manufacturer merely producing components; the judge who is only applying the law; the minister who is merely fulfilling the offices of state; the soldier who is carrying out orders: in all such cases, role responsibility, at least in terms of the most common and predominant cultural expectations, has the same effects. It segregates responsibility for role from responsibility for consequences; it legitimates the separation of intention from ultimate outcomes and does, indeed, offer the presumption of these persons' actions as both responsible *and* blameless. The fact that these forms are so very occasionally found to be deeply problematic—with such headline-making cases of an Eichmann or the East German border guards—merely shows up the fact that, in the normal run of things, they *do* carry the weight of justification that sees the question of responsibility successfully measured by role.

At one level at least, this is not some clandestine or hidden function that needs to be brought out into the light. Often role responsibilities are explicitly and publicly employed in professional and other forms precisely because there are thought to be good reasons for attaching immunities to particular roles, without which, it is usually maintained, that role would not be able to function properly (parliamentary privilege or the immunity of judges from suit in their capacity as judges, for example). Here, the role, status or office is deployed explicitly to deny or annul other potential responsibilities, even when harms may directly ensue.

Yet this function is far more deeply ingrained and widespread than the existence of these formal instantiations would seem to suggest. It extends beyond such openly justified immunities to the point at which the multiplication of role responsibilities results in a culture of impunity precisely under conditions where increasingly 'we have entrusted important parts of our lives . . . to *professional keepers of responsibility*' (Petersen, 2000, p 3, emphasis added). In such circumstances, and given the very obvious fact that the basic elements of the reproduction of social life rely almost entirely upon the division of labour, the point is reached at which there is an omnivorous tendency for role responsibilities to cover more and more of the field of responsibility as such. What is remarkable, then, is not the *exceptionality* of the immunities and disaggregations that these formal roles are capable of providing, but that their functional equivalents are, under such circumstances, ubiquitous. And ironically, all of the dependencies and expectations that come with the increasing deployment of role responsibilities and various other 'responsibilization strategies' (Garland, 1996) are no doubt linked to the very fragmented nature of responsibility practices themselves. With the rise of the division of labour of *responsibilities* themselves, and their organisation within multiple roles and institutions, the quest for responsibility arises simultaneously with the reality that organised *irresponsibility* is the overall effect of these features and their proliferation. And this is particularly so the *greater* the amount of harm produced, as our examples so far—and as we will see further later—tend to show. For as Bauman's work demonstrated—and the features it identified are, of course, endemic to modern social systems—*how else* do we explain activities that can be, and are, so devastating in their effects, but so negligible in their registering in terms of responsibility?

Hence we begin more fully to comprehend the claim that the existence of irresponsibility is effected through the organisation of responsibilities, where irresponsibility in light of the conditions just noted refers not only to disregard for consequences (that is, that actors need not look beyond the role to the full nature and effects of the enterprise), but also legitimate disregard of the possibility that it is the pursuit and validation of the role itself that can and does *cover up* the very question of responsibility. This, again, exemplifies the more profound sense discussed before: that, from the perspective of our opening asymmetry between the production of harms and establishing responsibility for them, we see how responsibility for harms vanishes in a proliferation of responsibilities, whereby suffering and alternative forms of responsibility may be legitimately disavowed through invoking the 'normative device' of role responsibility. Yet on this understanding, such occurrences are not to be taken as chaotic, as an unfortunate oversight or excess, but rather as structured immunity, as organised impunity. As such they *cohere* with—in fact, they are given impetus by—the very commonplace organisational forms of modern Western societies. As Bauman put it in the context of the Holocaust, this entails an acknowledgement—one so frequently, deeply and so tellingly *resisted*—that 'the Holocaust-style phenomena must be recognized as legitimate outcomes of civilizing tendency, and its constant potential' (Bauman, 1989, p 28).

Disclaimers of involvement are therefore put in place through, among other things, the disaggregation of roles, setting up a complex apartheid of responsibilities that furthers and legitimates the possibilities of disavowal. And thus we come to the most profound implication: the perpetuation of harm and suffering may come about *not* through so many broken promises, but rather through something far more disturbing, its opposite—promises fulfilled, bargains kept and *jobs well done*.

Role responsibilities form one of the most prevalent and profound ways of 'disappearing' responsibility, not only because this form of responsibility is so widespread—in ways that are centrally important also to law, as we will see later—but because it covers its tracks so well and in such mundane ways. Analogously to the horizontal/vertical nature of the division of labour, responsibilities may disappear likewise along both axes, as is perhaps most obvious when viewed in terms of sanctions attaching to the role that confirm certain routine expectations. On the one hand, the further up the chain of command or corporate hierarchy, the less likely is responsibility to be attached; because of the number of diversionary practices and structural dispersions that may be employed—including, for example, lack of causal connection or knowledge, but also the deployment of time as a delaying mechanism—those in directing or supervisory positions are often difficult to pin down in ways that would connect harm with their alleged responsibility. On the other hand, even if a connection can be made, it is commonly perceived that it is impossible to establish what, if any, consequences would be commensurate with the harms initiated or planned. (This is why there so often tends to be an operational asymmetry occurring here regarding the legitimation of an inversely proportional variation in the gravity of sanction: for the soldier or worker on the ground, say, responsibility for harms might entail imprisonment, shaming or job loss; at the top, with the minister or chief executive, it might mean simply resignation from office or loss of bonus. While there are truly countless examples of this asymmetry, the very rare exceptions to it that may get some publicity merely show up the normal expectation of the asymmetry itself.) So prevalent and *widely accepted* are these that they are often explained as being (with some due measure of 'regret', whatever that means given that it usually amounts to nothing) 'just the way things are', and so inured to the often massive asymmetries they allow are they that it is usually forgotten just what they *do*, in fact, legitimate.

We might note in passing that this is also why, for those tempted to take a consequentialist stance with regard to harms and who seek to look beyond the role to the actual consequences of the action, the difficulty is really no less. The problem still comes down to this: *who* should be held responsible for any, or all, consequences (and for which consequences), *given* the mediated and mediating nature of the production of harms? We are no further forward with this set of problems, because we have to return immediately to all of the structures and disaggregations that we have just described, and for which, as Bovens (1998, p 4) puts it: 'With respect to complex organisations . . . turns the quest for responsibility into a quest for the Holy Grail.'

That social action is so heavily reliant on role responsibilities for the organisation of its elementary functions, and that so many of these are necessary for the production or fulfilment of basic goods and needs, largely explains why, when they do produce 'bads' of the most extensive kind—*as only these forms of organisation can do*—there is an almost overwhelming reluctance to explore further, to open up to critical scrutiny these very practices and their institutional formations. Indeed, it is often not simply a reluctance, but an *inability* to do so, because these practices are constitutive of the very conditions of routine action and agents' self-understanding in the first place.

And where this is so, this deep resilience is a key reason why the putative role of alternative sources of normativity—such as belief in a critical morality—and their priority in social action and its consequences is effectively limited. Because it is necessary to see also that, within these structural forms and role responsibilities, not only can, say, *moral* understandings be manipulated, shifted around and put out of view in a variety of tactical ways according to the numerous technologies of responsibility, but that any such claimed understandings themselves may have no plausible appearance whatever. Again, as Milgram observed:

> Values are not the only forces at work in an actual, ongoing situation. They are but one narrow band of causes in the total spectrum of forces impinging on a person . . . Moral factors can be shunted aside with relative ease by a calculated restructuring of the informational and social field.
>
> (Milgram, 1974, pp 6–7)

This insight relates directly to the kinds of practices and techniques noted earlier, and confirms the importance of understanding the fuller sociological implications of these forces of 'calculated restructuring' with which we have just been concerned. It also confirms a point made at the end of the previous section about how dubious it may be to see moral claims as forms of communication that have any priority. If it is the case that morality can be 'managed', as Bauman puts it, in and through these structures, then it is also true that its claims and the theorising that attend them are also deeply implicated in the forms and processes we have just described, precisely to the extent that they fail to reflexively grasp these social conditions.

Nothing attests to this better than that *these* insights—of the kind that Bauman and Milgram offer—tend to be routinely disconnected from (academic and social) discourses of moral and political *principle*, a fact that is itself, ironically, all too symptomatic of the division of labour that is precisely what is at issue in all of this.

Yet when we start, as I suggested earlier, from the perspective of suffering, the general conclusion that Bauman offers serves as a startling indictment of the potential and realities of the processes outlined in this section:

> . . . the outcomes of our action and inaction reach far beyond the limits of our moral imagination and our readiness to assume responsibility for the weal and woe of the people whose lives have been directly or indirectly affected. This is why our shared capacity to do harm seems infinitely greater than our shared capacity to do good.
>
> (Bauman, 2002, p 214)

Individualisation and the irresponsible mentality

The second main feature to turn to also emerges from something touched upon earlier. In this instance, it concerns directly the anxiety we referred to through Calasso (1994): that the modern individual, proud of his responsibility, is not even sure with which voice he speaks. We now need to make sense of this in the context of trying to come to grips with how one of the highpoints of the achievements of modernity—the individual—in fact needs to be better understood through the process of 'individualisation' under contemporary social conditions. We can deal with this more briefly, since it draws on several of the sociological observations just made and is, in a sense, an intensification of these. The purpose of looking at this discretely through the lens of individualisation is, however, twofold. On the one hand, building on the observations about role responsibilities in the previous section, our aim is to understand how the nature of the individual is currently overdetermined by the systemic conditions within, and by, which it is constituted. If the figure of the individual helped to energise the transition into modernity, and if its spirit still propels the rhetoric of a dominant liberal political and moral philosophy and its language of rights and responsibilities, then the social order that sustains these ideals at one and the same time radically undermines their practical plausibility. At the same time as the celebrated figure of the modern individual emerged, modern Western society entered an era of unprecedented institutional power shifts that saw the individual increasingly subject to forces over which it had no control. In an important sense, the predominance and superficiality of individual *choice*, I will suggest, appears as a telling symptom of these widespread developments. On the other hand, then, our aim is to show how these features connect to a more widespread culture, or mentality, of irresponsibility. In this way, we can again sharpen our perceptions of how the disappearance of responsibilities in the context of large-scale, and legally authorised, suffering continues. Hence the matter of individualisation is significant in itself, but also serves, as we will see, to highlight more general concerns.

Mark Bovens (1998) points to the major discrepancy, or asymmetry, that modern societies embody at their core as existing 'between the enlightenment ideal of the autonomous individual and the social reality of dominant bureaucratic organisations'. What is new, he suggests, about the structure and organisation of modern societies is 'above all the fact that the asymmetry is no longer between individuals, but between two fundamentally different types of actors: people and complex organisations' (Bovens, 1998, pp 10, 19). Now, if it is contestable that prior forms of asymmetry are, in fact, best understood as conflicts between individuals—rather than between classes, or nations, or whatever—it is undoubtedly the case that contemporary social relations are dominated by complex organisations and the systemic dynamics in which they operate (some of which were identified in the previous section). But these forms have a special significance for the meaning of agency itself. If the larger scale phenomena we have just been discussing make for a more complex, detailed picture within which responsibility and its disavowals need to be situated, then they also impact directly on the understandings and possibilities for individual and collective action. Here, in other words, agency needs again to be situated in a force field of more or less structurally articulated contexts that bear on the meaning of 'individuals' and their social relations. While, at one level, this may appear an uncontroversial observation, how it plays out in practice is crucial.

Let me now draw on one reading of this in order to set out the problematic. Ulrich Beck's analysis (1992) of the risk society—to which we will return in more detail in a later chapter—includes an important discussion of the notion of 'individualisation'. Set within the broad trajectory of modernity, in contemporary Western capitalist societies, it is, argues Beck, increasingly the case that: 'The individual him or herself becomes the reproduction unit for the social in the lifeworld.' But the processes of 'individualisation' that this involves rely at one and the same time on the achievements of a number of social systems and institutions, which employ processes of *standardisation*.

This creates, he says, a situation of 'novel character', which he calls 'the contradictory double face of institutionally dependent individual situations':

> The apparent outside of the institutions becomes the inside of individual biography. The design of life situations spanning institutional boundaries results from their institutional dependency (in the broadest sense). The liberated individuals become dependent on the labour market and *because of that*, dependent on education, consumption, welfare state regulations and support, traffic planning, consumer supplies, and on possibilities and fashions in medical, psychological and pedagogical counselling and care. This all points to the *institution-dependent control structure* of individual situations. Individualization becomes the *most advanced* form of socialization dependent on the market, law, education and so on.
>
> (Beck, 1992, pp 130–1)

The significance of this contradictory feature manifests itself in ways that expose, in now more pronounced form, the 'ambiguity' to which Calasso (1994) drew our attention: '[I]t is precisely individualized private existence which becomes more and more obviously and emphatically dependent on situations and conditions that completely escape its reach.' In other words, 'Individualization thus takes effect precisely under general social conditions which allow an individual autonomous private existence even less than before' (Beck, 1992, p 131).

Yet despite this *diminution* in autonomy, albeit paradoxically structured in terms of individualisation, enormous pressure is placed on *individuals* to perceive themselves as masters of their fate. Thus, as Beck explains it:

> an ego-centred world view *must* be developed . . . The institutional conditions that determine individuals are no longer just events and conditions that happen to them, but also consequences of the decisions they themselves have made, which they must view and treat as such . . . Everything which appears separated in the perspective of systems theory, becomes an integral component of the individual biography: family *and* wage labour, education *and* employment, administration *and* the transport system, consumption, pedagogy, and so on.

On this reading, the very reality of systemic forms and their potential contradictions produces individuals who are simultaneously taken to be the mainspring of meaning and tossed around by contradictory forces. Hence, for Beck, the final paradox (1992, pp 136–7): 'At the same moment as he or she sinks into insignificance, he or she is elevated to the apparent throne of world-shaper.'

In some respects, it has been argued, the liberal mindset, the liberal personality of modern Western capitalist society, is the most problematic instantiation of this because it fulfils this paradoxical condition expertly, by internalising choices given from outside and making them its own. In many ways, this was precisely the insight that Foucault's work (1983) on disciplinary power and the technologies of the self provided in such a nuanced, but cogent, manner. What these analyses showed was that 'processes of subjectivization bring the individual to bind himself to his own identity and consciousness and, at the same time, to an external power'. It is in this way, according to Agamben's reading of Foucault, that 'the modern Western state has integrated techniques of subjective individualization with procedures of objective totalization to an unprecedented degree' (1998, p 5).

As well as the state, of course, societal processes of individualisation, generally, introduce a problematic of identity and agency that is not persuasively understood solely in human terms. (This will be of particular significance in a different context when we consider questions of citizens' complicity in government actions later.) Where the individual is an *outcome*—of complex and contradictory systemic demands and stakes—then the attribution of freedom, responsibility, capacity, etc. to the individual is inevitably bound up with an understanding of *these* demands and stakes. And to the extent that these systemic forms (including, although not only, those identified in the previous section) are able to shift around meanings of responsibility and hence to produce zones of non-responsibility in the ways we have seen, then the notion of the individual likewise embodies these characteristics— and not only superficially, but at its core. Here, to put it in different terms, the mentality of responsibility—the desired productions of the different forms of responsibility practices—co-originates and co-exists with the mentality of irresponsibility that these also produce, thus producing a personality not of alienated being—alienated from what?—but of *identity*, so to speak, constituted by this very multiple or split mentality.

On this understanding, the person can be entirely separated neither from his or her social locations and roles among the competing systemic demands Beck identified, nor from *personality*, which is, of course, a cultural, rather than personal, achievement. It almost goes without saying that, since the social *relation* is no more inured to this because it too faces technical forms and systemic demands, processes of individualisation are inescapably *productive* of subjectivities *and* relations themselves.

Now the effect of these insights may be thought to be chilling: what they point to is summed up (albeit the conclusion is reached via a different route) by Alasdair MacIntyre (1985) in his description of the 'emotivist' nature of contemporary culture under the kind of conditions we have just been noting. The most significant impact of these, he argues, is that 'the contrast between power and authority, although paid lip-service to, is effectively obliterated as a special instance of the *disappearance of the contrast between manipulative and non-manipulative social relations*' (MacIntyre, 1985, p 26, emphasis added). If the Kantian ideal in modernity was that individuals were, in Kant's famous dictum, to be treated as autonomous ends in themselves and never as means, then, according to MacIntyre, this 'Enlightenment project' has failed. Such autonomy as there is now expresses itself most emphatically *not* as the self-determining autonomous subject, but as the focal point of so many choices to be made, choices that are set out only within the parameters of the options made available according to the logic of the dominant social systems—work choices; health choices; identity choices; insurance choices; and hence, most decisively (for all of these choices sooner or later come to be expressed in these terms), consumer choices. Where this has indeed become the dominant form of subjectivity—and who could plausibly deny this to be the case for hyper-consumerist Western culture?—then Kant's ambitious autonomous moral subject is reduced to the reality of a self as 'chooser between pre-given options', for whom therefore there is no 'autonomy' that is not already manipulated or manipulable. As MacIntyre puts it, this self 'which has no necessary social content and no necessary social identity can then be anything, can assume any role or take any point of view, because it *is* in and for itself nothing' (MacIntyre, 1985, p 32, emphasis in original). Since individuals are constituted in and as the attribution point of the logic of social systems and institutions under conditions of individualisation, and because they are not only subject to, but subjects *of*, these needs and demands, the distinction between manipulative and non-manipulative social relations disappears and the modern individual, rather than being an end in itself, has all the real autonomy of a swimmer's body in rough seas.

Yet for all that, as Beck noted, paradoxically this has not lessened the demands on the individual to *appear* to be autonomous. Appearance, however, is not the reality. As Zizek (2001b, p 8) pointedly asks: 'Are not the basic characteristics of today's "postmodern" subject . . . the exact opposite of the free subject who experiences himself as ultimately responsible for his fate?' With this observation, we are jolted back to the possibility that the presence of the old 'gods' and their effects on human actions as Calasso so eloquently described them, have, despite everything, merely been replaced by new ones. Responsibility did not trouble the Homeric heroes in the same way as it does the moderns—but that does not leave the latter untroubled either. The modern fixation with responsibility, freedom, intention and liability devolves on human relations as encountered through individual understandings and responses, but only as these are the mediated products of the totality of modernity's institutional and disciplinary achievements. And hence the anxiety: who is to say that the 'moderns' have not returned to a state of 'mental infirmity' that Calasso associated with the Homeric heroes, or that such an infirmity is not the very condition of modern responsibility? What it means to say that these choices—these so many choices—are those given only by the dominant forms of the institutions in place is that, by and large, there is no critical vantage point that can be reached that is *not already implicated in these*. There is no choice not to choose apart from the options on offer and this, again, reinforces the fact that the distinction between manipulative and non-manipulative relations disappears, because choices, personalities, roles, etc. are geared to logics and disciplines that are not those which respect autonomy as such (that is, in itself). The distinction then disappears, or is, as MacIntyre suggests, *obliterated*, because to respect the individual as *other* than chooser only among pre-given terms, individual action—even collective action—would have to be able to burst the bounds of these forms to be true to itself. Only if it could, might the distinction be maintained. But under current conditions, this does not appear to be an available choice.

That this—we might call it—radical quietism has come to be so prevalent today is, in many ways, not so surprising given what was noted earlier: that, through processes of individualisation, the modern self has already internal- ised these *as* its (only) options. Busy with its choices, the modern Western 'individualised' self does not, cannot, see conflict as genuinely incommensur- able or tragic because there is nothing that will be beyond all measure, noth- ing that will not be able to be dealt with through the right form of social treatment: the right policy; the right product; the right therapy; the right price. On another view, of course, this is precisely the tragedy *of* the modern subject: that it cannot see this. So confident and proud of its responsibilities, and yet—with all of its deep reliances, its confident anxieties—also so pro- foundly uncertain about these, suggesting perhaps that the modern obsession with all of the numerous forms of responsibility is some, no matter how distant, index of precisely these. (By contrast, one cannot imagine the tragic heroes sitting around agonising over these fine distinctions of responsibility that the modern taxonomies offer. 'This is no time for fine distinctions,' says Creon in Jean Anhouilh's version of the *Antigone*—and yet contemporary life is *replete* with them.)

Hence we come finally to what I have termed the 'irresponsible mentality'. To get a sense of this, we might consider by way of a comparison one of the key preoccupations of the work of Isaiah Berlin: namely, the critique of philosophical and political monism. According to the monist mentality, there exists an 'urge to shed the burden of responsibility for one's fate by transfer- ring it to a vast impersonal monolithic whole—"nature, or history, or class or race, or the 'harsh realities of our time', or the irresistible evolution of the social structure, that will absorb and integrate us into its limitless, indifferent, neutral texture, which it is senseless to evaluate or criticise, and against which we fight to our certain doom"' (Kelly, 1979, p xv, quoting Berlin, 1969). Berlin's sense was that this mentality, which had come to dominate so much of twentieth-century political and social life, had intellectual, but also deeply human, roots and lay in the eagerness 'to trade the doubts and agonies of moral responsibility for determinist visions, conservative or radical' (Kelly, 1979, p xvi). Berlin's rejection of this lay in the claim that it was 'the greatest of sins that any human being can perpetrate[:] to seek to transfer moral responsibility from his own shoulders to an unpredictable future order' (ibid, quoting Berlin).

This aspect of the monist mentality is clear enough: a dissolving of individual (moral) responsibility in the monist solvent, the resultant solution of which is always apparently irreversible and, from Berlin's point of view, dangerous, because it 'treats heterodoxy as the supreme danger' (Berlin, 1969, p 38). This (dis)solution absorbs and absolves individual responsibility largely through the great ideological promises that are on offer, be they left or right, and with it disappear, he says, the troubles of 'agonizing moral conflict', which are *eliminated* in favour of a simpler and *better regulated life*, a robust faith in an *efficiently working order*' (ibid, emphasis added). Now it is less the grand ideological absolution in which we are interested here—its history reaches far back beyond modernity—but rather the latter phrases of this final observation. These point us to a second sense in which an 'irresponsible mentality' is identifiable, one discovered not at the level of ideas or ideologies, but at the level of the very mundane operation of the structural forms that have come to dominate contemporary Western society (and the relevance of which cuts across both monist and pluralist approaches). According to this, the dissolution of responsibility will not be in terms of class, or nation, or race, or whatever, but will follow decisively from a total immersion in the 'solutions' of social structures and in the 'rational' ordering of social systems to the demands and expectations of which (ironically, in Berlin's terms) it is impossible to impute a single coherent purpose or ideology. In these structures, we find the irresponsible mentality in the formation and limitation of characters, roles, choices, and the system-specific nature of agency, action and expectations, the combined, although unintended, effect of which is precisely of the type Berlin identified: namely, the 'urge to shed the burden of responsibility for one's fate', not now to the 'monolithic whole', but to the plurality of social systems, and their offerings and solutions, whatever they might be—consumer economy; administrative decision making; accounting and auditing; educational (teaching and research) assessments, etc.; all of these measurements and more.

Overall and within this plurality of forms, the 'individual' modern subject—and most especially that of the individual as consumer—and its responsibilities are readily dissolved in the wash of the, at once totalising and 'liberating', experience of the social structures and their roles, the categories and priorities of which are so deeply ingrained that they are taken as 'our own' choices and responsibilities. In this, the disappearance of the distinction between manipulative and non-manipulative social relations entails that responsibility and its obliteration—irresponsibility—go hand in hand according to the logics and priorities not of autonomous individuals, but of the systems they serve to reproduce. As ever, of course, the genius of this occurrence is that it appears otherwise than it is. Indeed, so profoundly internalised are the expectations of this 'irresponsible mentality' that they are taken, as Nietzsche had predicted, as natural, as instinct—indeed, as an instinct of responsibility! In a recent essay on responsibility, John Gardner (2003) captures this particularly well (no doubt unintentionally, because it is a claim unclouded by sociological curiosity and all the more telling for that) when he writes that 'it is part of our nature' that:

> We all want our wrongs and mistakes to have been justified. Failing that, we want them to have been excused. No sooner have we noticed that we did something wrong or mistaken than we start rolling out our justifications and excuses.
>
> (Gardner, 2003, p 157)

Here, precisely, is the mark of modern responsibility, at one and the same time embodying the mentality of irresponsibility as it rolls out all of 'our' justifications and excuses.

So we return, again, to our earlier asymmetry: the experiences of suffering are profoundly human, but the forms that enable their production are all mediated. There *are* human actors, but their actions are as nothing without the structures of government, hierarchy, bureaucracy and economy, and their attendant concepts (office, status, rationality and profit). It is these modern gods that engender the modern anxiety; as Calasso (1994) points out, they trouble us by asking: whose voice, what voice, speaks when 'we' speak? 'We' are not sure it is 'ours', or even what 'our' voice is. In this simultaneously exulted and emaciated condition, the moderns draw all of their distinctions of responsibility—between who is responsible and what is responsible; responsible to what and for whom, or for what and to whom; between who or what or whatever caused what—which, in all their permutations, may be secured or obliterated as required, while all the time the production of suffering continues.

In seeking to distinguish '*the evil of the mind and the evil of the deed, murder and death*', the moderns have gifted themselves a noble place for responsibility that contains, at one and the same time, all of the possibilities for its disavowal. Through all of the varied concepts and categories, distinctions and systems, institutions and disciplines in which the modern individual exists and operates can be found the modern tools for disconnecting effect and cause, liability and suffering, murder and death. It is such diversions that make sense and nonsense of the lives of modern individuals, which together *make sense* of the fact that, as Stanley Cohen (2001, p 294) puts it, 'the world of suffering makes moral imbeciles of us all'. And it is within these co-ordinates—temporal; spatial; individualised; institutional—that the normality of the asymmetries is maintained, and that the symbiotic mentalities of responsibility and irresponsibility need to be understood.

Responsibility transference—politics and economy

The third and final feature concerns the way in which social systems and their interactions themselves allow irresponsibility to proliferate through forms of responsibility transference. This issue has been lurking in the background so far and now needs to be brought to the fore. In this section, I concentrate on just one manifestation of this—namely, the interaction between the political and the economic, because this is central to understanding the problems with which the book is concerned. (In the next chapter, we look directly at how the law and the legal system are involved.) What I seek to describe here is, again, not some insight into some timeless nature of that relation, because such does not exist; rather, in providing some historical background, we need to understand how that relation works today in respect, on the one hand, of the predominant forms of the relation in the contemporary political and economic arrangements of modern capitalist societies, and, on the other, of their involvement in the production and legitimation of suffering.

In that sense, the task is again largely descriptive: it is to understand how the production of suffering is normalised through, what I term, the capabilities of responsibility transference. Hence it focuses on how dominant interpretations and legitimations of the political and economic spheres and their relation underpin the disappearance of responsibility through mechanisms that are geared to organising impunities in structural ways. In line with the general argument, then, the focus is not on the exceptional, but on the normal or, to be more precise, on how extensive suffering—in this section, we will consider specifically that which is associated with mass poverty in time of plenty—is to be understood not as an excess, but as the normal (or normalised) product of systems, the combination of which is working. It is in this respect—in this case, routine understandings of politics and economics—that we must understand the occurrence of the asymmetries between suffering and the inability to establish responsibility for it.

Let us begin, then, with a local example. In March 2007, two Scottish-based banks produced some excellent financial results. The Royal Bank of Scotland announced record annual profits of £9.2bn and, a few days later, Halifax Bank of Scotland recorded its own record-breaking amount of £6bn. Both sets of results were met with congratulations by 'the markets', the financial media and political sources: the devolved government in Edinburgh (as well, no doubt, as that in Westminster) was very pleased, it said, by the banks' successes.

In that same month, the government in Edinburgh, a Labour-led Scottish Executive, announced that there were '900,000 Scots living in poverty, 240,000 of them children' (Macwhirter, 2007, p 34), an increase of 20,000 on the previous year. In response, it noted that it was its priority to reduce by half the number of children living in poverty by 2010 and to seek to eradicate child poverty entirely by 2020.

Now, what is striking about these two sets of figures is that they co-exist in ways that, for the vast majority of people, make sense, or at least do not cause political or moral turmoil. My point here, I should say, is not a political one: it is about trying to understand how the suffering of poverty and particularly the—widely accepted—harm of child poverty exist together with such wealth. The appearance of mass poverty and extreme wealth co-exist, and do so comfortably within a small country (showing also how temporal and spatial distances and the irresponsible mentality do not only operate on a large canvas, for those harms occurring 'somewhere else'); no one—save the poor—is overly discomforted by this 'discrepancy', if indeed it is seen as such at all. All of the diversionary mechanisms are securely in place, it would seem, when it comes to the good folk of Scotland and their fine political and economic institutions.

In this, they are by no means exceptional, of course, because they operate within an intellectual and material heritage that appears to legitimate these kinds of 'discrepancies'. Here, for example, is how Jurgen Habermas (2005) recently described the general tendency. In a discussion of the 'egalitarian universalism of human rights', Habermas distinguished the level of 'conceptual relations' from the 'factual conditions that are deformed by violence':

> Naturally . . . liberal 'systems of equality' have generally covered up the flagrant injustices of social inequality . . . But these facts do not reveal a paradox rooted in the normativity of the idea of equality itself. Rather, the contradiction between the normative claim . . . and the morally obscene sight that they actually present merely produces cognitive dissonance.
>
> (Habermas, 2005, p 14)

For Habermas, then, liberal ideals—equality, justice, dignity or security—are not tarnished by the existence of things such as the '*morally obscene sight*' of extensive poverty in circumstances of extraordinary wealth; they '*merely*' produce cognitive dissonance. (Let us leave aside for now such obvious questions as: For *whom* exactly does this produce '*merely*' cognitive dissonance? What—and who—is preserved when we preserve the integrity of the ideals alone? From which perspective does it make sense to say that these ideals remain untouched by the fact of suffering? Why is the cover-up 'natural'?)

The situation in Scotland that I have just mentioned concerns, it should be pointed out, what is called 'relative' poverty. When we pan out our focus to the global level, the situation of poverty and wealth is vastly increased, and not only in terms of figures, but in terms of a shift to absolute poverty levels. In an era in which globalisation signifies, according to Giddens' definition, 'the intensification of worldwide social relations which link distant localities in such a way that local happenings are shaped by events occurring many miles away and vice versa' (quoted in Santos, 2002, p 165), then there is a very obvious sense in which the greatest of mass harms suffered today are those perpetuated through structures of economic immiseration within an interconnected global economy. The Scottish situation, bad as it is, pales by comparison with the extensive suffering occurring worldwide and the scale of which, in the context of abundance, is staggering. Such suffering is well documented, and the institutions and policies that maintain it are perfectly legal. They include some of the following proportions: over 1 billion people globally live on, or with less than, US$1 per day, a figure that refers to what $1 would buy in the USA. Another two and a half billion people are living on only US$2 per day, a figure that has increased by 50 per cent since 1980. Among the consequences of this poverty are: '14% of the world's population (826 million) are undernourished; 16% (968 million people) lack access to safe drinking water; 40% (2,400 million people) lack access to basic sanitation; 15% lack access to health services; and 17% have no adequate shelter and 33% no electricity.' Consequently, 'One third of all human deaths are due to poverty-related causes . . . all of which could be prevented or cured cheaply through food, safe drinking water, vaccinations, rehydration packs or medicine', and yet, since 1990, 250 million people, mainly children, have died from preventable diseases. (Figures and quotes in this paragraph are from Pogge, 2002, ch 4, and are sourced from recent UNICEF, World Bank and UN Development Programme reports.)

'This destitution persists', notes the World Bank, 'even though human conditions have improved more in the past century than in the rest of history—global wealth, global connections, and global technological capabilities have never been greater.' The problem is clear, however, even to the World Bank (2000–01, p 3): the distribution of gains is 'extraordinarily unequal. The average income in the richest 20 countries is 37 times the average in the poorest 20—a gap that has doubled in the last 40 years'. But extensive poverty on this scale is, we are led to believe (although never by those who suffer from its effects), a complex matter.

As these last figures show and as Pogge's work amply demonstrates, these harms are not, and ought not to be seen as, external to the dominant forces of global capitalism. The same is true today as it was for the cases of extensive poverty-related deaths of previous times: as Mike Davis (2001), for example, has written of the policies of British imperialism in causing the nineteenth-century famines in India and elsewhere:

> Millions died not outside the 'modern world system', but in the very process of being forcibly incorporated into its economic and political structures. They died in the golden age of Liberal Capitalism.
>
> (Davis, 2001, p 9)

In other words, both unprecedented 'improvements' and wealth *and* immiseration are outcomes of the *same* structures and processes, and are maintained through the diverse range of institutions that sustain global capitalism.

In order to make a little sense of how some of these occurrences appear to be legitimate, I consider only one aspect here, but this aspect is, I suggest, one of the key features underlying what Gunther Grass referred to when he suggested that 'Irresponsibility is the organizing principle of the neoliberal vision' (Grass and Bourdieu, 2002, p 71). This concerns the distinction between the political and economic, and, in the remainder of this chapter, I will set out the following: firstly, some historical dimensions to this relation and the way in which the ideal of an autonomous economic realm emerges; secondly, how it facilitates a form of political amnesia or disassociation through a form of depoliticisation that sets the terms for the obliteration of responsibility for massive harms (such as mass poverty in situations of increasing wealth); finally, how this position becomes entrenched in such a manner that even contemporary political theory, based on democratic principles of equality, fails to be able to overcome the distinction and, as such, largely explains the legitimation of suffering as part of the practice of democratic principle.

Let us begin with a brief consideration of the work of Karl Polanyi (1957), one of the most acute observers of the political, economic and cultural shifts that took place from the turn of the eighteenth into the nineteenth centuries and beyond. In his most important work, he argues that a great transformation occurred in the course of the nineteenth century, whereby a concerted attempt was made to institute the 'self-regulating market'. The principles of such a market, unlike those, say, of a command economy, were thought to respect the autonomy of individuals by refusing to treat them paternalistically—that is, refusing to assume that somebody knows better than they do how resources should be allocated to them. Moreover, since only the market actors themselves, it was argued, would have sufficient knowledge of their own desires and needs, such knowledge could not be centralised, either at all or, at the very least, efficiently. (These were, as Hayek (1944, pp 56–7) was later to encapsulate them, the moral and epistemological presuppositions on which free market principles are based.)

But the trouble with the market as understood in this way is that it fails, says Polanyi, to take account of the enormous institutional effort and ongoing enforcement required to inaugurate and sustain it. The free market ideal starts with the premise of natural liberty, and then treats the emergent forms and activities that enable it to flourish as a spontaneous development. But as Polanyi ably demonstrated, this is neither conceptually, nor historically, persuasive. There was no *spontaneous* ordering of this sort without extensive planning and centralisation of authority to hold the possibility of 'autonomous' market action in place. (The recent history of the development of a free market in the European Union is testimony enough to that.) Historically, then, the specific conditions necessary for establishing the institutionalisation of the self-regulating market—the institutionalisation of labour, land and money as commodities—required intensive organisation and force, which resulted in a profound social transformation and, with it, cultural dislocations of an unprecedented nature. Thus, despite the commonplace historical myth that has still not been entirely dislodged, the efforts to institute the self-regulating market might best be understood in the following paradoxical terms:

> While *laissez-faire* economy was the product of deliberate state action, subsequent restrictions on *laissez-faire* started in a spontaneous way. *Laissez-faire* was planned; planning was not.
>
> (Polanyi, 1957, p 141)

Despite having drawn inspiration from the economics of Adam Smith, the rise of the new discipline of free market economics marked a decisive shift away from Smith's own work. For Smith, moral action rooted in sympathy and benevolence was the basis of social relations, and economic action and its political settings were not separable from, but rather part of, an overall framework of human relations, which were to be understood as a greater unity. According to Polanyi's interpretation of Smith (1957, p 112): 'The dignity of man is that of a moral being, who is, as such, a member of the civic order of family, state, and the "great Society of mankind" . . .' Hence for Smith, wealth was:

> an aspect of the life of the community, to the purposes of which it remained subordinate . . . there is no intimation in his work that the economic interests of the capitalists laid down the law to society; no intimation that they were the secular spokesmen of the divine providence which governed the economic world as a separate entity. The economic sphere, for him, is not yet subject to laws of its own that provide us with a standard of good and evil . . . In [Smith's] view nothing indicates the presence of an economic sphere that might become the source of moral law and political obligation.
>
> (Polanyi, 1957, pp 111–12)

By the middle of the nineteenth century, however—and due, paradoxically enough, in no small degree to the attraction of Smith's economic analyses—a divorce did take place that separated the economy from its social locations in a highly specific manner. The sense in which Smith had understood the role of economy gave way to the new form of the recognisably modern capitalist understanding, and, in *this* form, the economy was treated as resting not on social and moral foundations, but rather the relation was reversed. Where economics came to be understood as primarily based on self-interest treated as a natural phenomenon, then a decisive change came about when, in the new post-Smith 'political economy', this civic dimension dropped away and instead self-interest was made to appear the foundation of civil society. With this, as Polanyi points out, 'The acceptance of a separate economic sphere . . .

implied the recognition of the principle of gain and profit as *the* organizing force in society' and, as such, 'Economic society had emerged as distinct from the political state' (Polanyi, 1957, pp 114–15, 170, emphasis added).

Now, despite the fact that the modern state and its politics are preoccupied with economic policies, the cleavage between the economic and the political spheres that had occurred through the assertion of an autonomous economic realm was of profound and enduring consequence. In order to link it directly to our current concerns, we might think about it in terms of *constituency*. At the political level of the state, equality of civil, political and even social rights as they emerged in the course of the nineteenth and twentieth centuries guaranteed a form of equality—the political constituency of citizens as equals before the law—that was absent in earlier periods. But these developments co-existed with the simultaneous constitution of the economic 'constituency' as a separate realm. Marx noted the effect of this disjunction in an early work. Asking whether the electoral freedom that came with the end of property qualifications on voting rights meant that the masses had now gained control over those with financial wealth, he wrote that:

> the political annulment of private property does not mean the abolition of private property; on the contrary, it presupposes it. The state in its own way abolishes distinctions based on *birth, rank, education* and *occupation* when it declares birth, rank, education and occupation to be *non-political* distinctions, when it proclaims that every member of the people is an equal participant in popular sovereignty regardless of these distinctions, when it treats all those elements which go to make up the actual life of the people from the standpoint of the state. Nevertheless the state allows private property, education and occupation to *act* and assert their *particular* nature in *their* own way, i.e., as private property, as education and as occupation. Far from abolishing these *factual* distinctions, the state presupposes them in order to exist, it only experiences itself as a *political state* and asserts its *universality* in opposition to these elements.
>
> (Marx, 1975, p 219, emphasis in original)

For Marx, voting rights based on universal suffrage rather than on a property qualification clearly saw the introduction of a form of equality in the make-up of the political constituency at the level of the state. But in doing so, that had the effect of *depoliticising* the economic constituency (and its influential social practices, reproduced in a range of fora such as occupations and education), which continued, nonetheless, to structure and maintain exploitative material relations. (As Marx put it, people were not given freedom from property or the 'egoism' of trade; they received freedom *of* property and freedom *to* trade.) Thus, despite the emergence and rise of what is called 'political economy', the term is, in many respects, misleading or oxymoronic:

the occurrence of the historical divorce meant that the forum of political principle, with its ideals of equality, freedom and citizenship, was *not* co-extensive with the economic realm and its practices of domination, exploit-ation and insecurity.

Political and economic identity are held apart, and the idea of participation or representation in the two realms are treated as disconnected achievements, despite the enormous impact of the latter on people's daily life experiences. So, to put it in contemporary terms for example, major *economic* actors such as domestic and international organisations and corporations are, on one view, undoubtedly political in so far as they are involved in the organisation of communities of participation and exclusion, agenda setting on matters of collective action, and in the delivery of normative frameworks and sanctions; yet these do not *register* as political activities, nor—crucially—as subject to the same demands of political justification, because they do not correspond to the state and its party political model. In this way, equality thought of as political equality guaranteed by the state under the rule of law may operate to legitimise and, as Marx argued, depend upon the existence and legitimisation of inequality. The mismatch between political equality and material inequal-ity thus continues to underpin key structures of social and economic life, while at the same time operating to limit the possibilities of the political constituency itself.

It is in this sense that we might think of the economic realm as being depoliticised: not in the sense that the treatment of what was once 'political' is now treated as non-political (a temporal sense), but of immunising from the reach of politics—by making it appear 'natural'—that which might, from other perspectives, be thought politically contestable. In this way, the fact that the two realms are treated in different ways makes possible the betrayal of the promise of a more thoroughgoing equality by setting limits to the possi-bilities for political action, when understood in these terms. And so it is in precisely this sense that the 'normal' disjunction between politics and eco-nomics can operate to facilitate the keeping in place of material benefits *and* structures of immiseration, while at the same time claiming victory for the equalities of the political constituency.

As such, the underlying problems of suffering consequent on the economic realm may never fully be exposed to the light of political contestation *except*, that is, to the extent that the contestation is made within, and congruent to, the terms of the already existing political institutions. But where this is so, the difficulty of having these harms register faces the challenge of trying to establish that which is denied—or least deniable—by the systems that are implicated in their existence. More prosaically, what the terms of political discourse will see as an economic problem, the economic system will see as a political one (if, indeed, it sees it all); in switching responsibility from one to the other, the problem of responsibility for suffering can be legitimately avoided. In this way, harms—which are themselves in no way disaggregated in experience—can be classified into separate categories and responsibility for them disappeared.

Yet it may still be argued that, despite an acknowledgement of a separation of the two systems in terms of types of legitimation, it is still plausible to see an overall, if not a combined, legitimation as both desirable and feasible—in particular, that is, to hold to account the economic realm in the political. James Tully (2002), for example, notes that many practices of governance— such as, he says, property systems, bureaucracies, markets, families, etc.— explicitly do not rely for their legitimacy on political principles such as democracy or constitutionalism. This is undoubtedly correct. But still, he goes on to argue:

> ... it does mean that if a system of cooperation is not organised democratically and constitutionally, then it requires a public justification that can be made good to the people who are subject to it and its effects (justifications such as efficiency, competency, utility, a distinction between public and private, tradition and so on).
>
> (Tully, 2002, p 210)

These justifications must be open to 'democratic disagreement and deliberation'.

Revealing as this seems, at first sight, an argument such as this overlooks the points about constituency that we have just been making and does so, in particular, because it fails properly to acknowledge the actual nature of certain forms of 'co-operation', the essence of which lies precisely in *circumscribing* collective co-operation, and which even depends on *negating* the possibility of having its justifications opened to democratic deliberation and disagreement. Nowhere is this truer than for certain key aspects of a capitalist economy. As well as—perhaps even underpinning—the moral and epistemological arguments alluded to earlier with reference to Hayek, consider the following points.

The first concerns the property form on which capitalist economies rely at their core (I will come back to some legal aspects of this in the next chapter). This takes its most powerful form in what Roberto Unger (1987, p 131) calls the 'consolidated property right', which engenders—and the language is such that it fits precisely with our general analysis—two powerful and inseparable *immunities*: one against the state; the other, in the form of 'power to set terms to others people's activities'. In more detail, the first entails a range of entitlements that create 'an island of security against the predatory or reformist actions of the state, a haven in which some material or ideal interest, and the actual person who is its bearer, can hide'. The effective function of this immunity is that it 'immobilizes a parcel of the state's capacity to move and shake the social world'. Such an immunity clearly has a long and well-established historical creed, reaching back as it does to the English 'glorious' revolution and its Lockean impetus, in terms of the natural right to property that governments must respect.

The second aspect Unger describes concerns either the direct power to 'define social status' or the indirect power to achieve entitlements over time 'by creating devices through which some become dependent on others' (1987, p 131). By the latter, Unger refers, among other things, to the protection of accumulated property by hereditary entitlement, the conditions for buying and selling labour, and, generally, the control of work and work conditions through organisational forms on which succeeding generations of workers are made dependent. The important point about these for now is that, once institutionalised and given various 'levels of sanctification', these immunities set definite *limits* on the terms according to which any supervisory or accountability function will be legitimate. That is, *pace* Tully's observation, they will colonise the terms and conditions on which the matters of deliberation and judgement will, and can only, take place *so long as* that general property form remains in existence. Thus, even in democracies, the system of powers and immunities necessitates that governments 'not go too far in favouring mass militancy and mass organization. The citizen participates. But he participates in a state whose ability to revise the terms of collective existence is highly limited' (Unger, 1987, p 133).

Not only this, but—forcefully, and ironically—these very *limits* set by the immunities of the property form will, as Locke famously argued, themselves be justified as the precondition *of* freedom at all. In this way, the ideals of political equality and freedom are able to *justify* the reality of massive inequality, which constitutes not only, as Habermas (2005) suggested, 'cognitive dissonance', but something far deeper: a form of conceptual amnesia, we might say, which has the separation of the economic and political irremovably at its root. That is, if political institutions are deemed to be based on public democratic deliberation and consent, consent in the economic realm is reduced only to meaning the freedom to exchange labour for wages and the choices of consumption, corresponding to the twin pillars of economic freedom in the democratic polity: free labour and the free market. On this model, the claim for political democracy and the forgetting of economic democracy go hand in hand: what is no longer free is the ability to redefine economic freedom; what is no longer a matter of consent is the meaning of economic consent. Each has been trapped in terms of the free market model and referred to by the political realm as non-political.

In this sense, the asymmetry in the political and the economic relation shows, again, that Tully's claim about democratic supervision will be unequal to the task proposed for it. The reason why is perhaps best summed up by Polanyi's observation that, where labour has become a commodity, has become defined in purely economic terms, then:

> It is not for the commodity to decide where it should be offered for sale, to what purpose it should be used, at what price it should be allowed to change hands, and in what manner it should be consumed or destroyed.
>
> (Polanyi, 1957, p 176)

That will be left to the judgement of the market, the responsibility of which is to economic value and not to democratic accountability. In such a way, the desired democratic legitimation will always be left constitutively in deficit. No one summed this up better than the economist Milton Friedman, who famously observed, *contra* those who would seek to make a rampant corporate sector socially responsible, that the social responsibility of corporations is to make profits.

Perhaps our best account of this takes us back, again, to Adam Smith who, in a striking passage, discerns the emergence of the inability to transfer accountability or responsibility from one realm to another. With a 'realist's indiscretion' (to use Tawney's lovely phrase), he noted the problem as it crystallised as a matter of differential appearance and representation; a problem that might be grasped symptomatically in terms of audibility or its lack: the silence of capitalists (the masters) and clamour of the workers:

> We rarely hear, it has been said, of the combinations of masters; though frequently of those of workmen. But whoever imagines, upon this account, that masters rarely combine, is as ignorant of the world as of the subject. Masters are always and every where in a sort of tacit, but constant and uniform combination, not to raise the wages of labour above their actual rate . . . We seldom, indeed, hear of this combination, because it is the usual, and one may say, the natural state of things which nobody ever hears of. . . . Such combinations, however, are frequently resisted by a contrary defensive combination of the workmen . . . [and] *they* are always abundantly heard of. In order to bring the point to a speedy decision, they have always recourse to the loudest clamour, and sometimes to the most shocking violence and outrage. They are desperate, and act with the folly and extravagance of desperate men, who must either starve, or frighten their masters into an immediate compliance with their demands.
>
> (Smith, 1976, p 84)

Here we have precisely the appearance of the contingent—economic exploitation—as fixed, indeed as the '*natural state*', and any reaction against it therefore as '*unnatural*' or '*outrageous*'. Had Smith stopped there, he would not fully have grasped the point about how these assumptions feed into the political realm in *entirely different* ways and the consequences that this has. But he immediately noted the response, in turn, to the noisy clamour of the workers:

The masters upon *these* occasions are just as clamorous upon the other side, and never cease to call aloud for the assistance of the civil magistrate, and the rigorous execution of those laws which have been enacted with so much severity against the combinations of servants, labourers, and journeymen. The workmen, accordingly, very seldom derive any advantage from the violence of those tumultuous combinations, which, partly from the interposition of the civil magistrate, partly from the superior steadiness of the masters, partly from the necessity which the greater part of the workmen are under of submitting for the sake of present subsistence, generally end in nothing, but the punishment or ruin of the ringleaders.

> (Smith, 1976, pp 84–5, emphasis added)

Generally still as true today as it was then, this observation illuminates wonderfully the hopeless optimism of the argument that Tully (2002) makes once the separation of the political and economic realms is entrenched, and where the latter is grounded in the (apparently natural) elements of the commodity and private property form. As such, supervisory responsibilities cannot be transferred to the political realm on terms that allow it to address that on which it, in fact, depends.

All of this might be seen to be overblown were it not for the normality of the existence of the kinds of extensive suffering that we noted at the start of this section, that produces ongoing mass immiseration associated with poverty and which is, at one and the same time, consequent on a global economy generating unprecedented wealth. What I have tried to show here is one, albeit important, aspect of how harms suffered remain unaccounted for through the immunities established in the relations between politics and economics, immunities assigned and transferred in such a way that the suffering continues *despite* the commitment to equality and to its alleviation. Because what is perhaps most striking of all about the political and economic arrangements as they stand under these conditions is this: that this asymmetry, between extensive suffering—amounting to millions of deaths *monthly* in an interconnected and abundant world—and the ability to establish responsibility for this suffering in *no way* provokes a belief that there is a crisis.

Indeed, it is not even clear, as I suggested earlier, that there is a 'cognitive dissonance' for those who do not suffer these ravages; rather, the standard political line in response is given clear expression by Ronald Dworkin (2000), a prominent liberal political and legal theorist. In a recent important work on equality, he argued that 'No government is legitimate that does not show equal concern for the fate of all those citizens over whom it claims dominion and from whom it claims allegiance' (Dworkin, 2000, p 1), a statement that, although abstract, is one that would, I expect, meet with the general approval of most contemporary theorists and practitioners of democratic government, for whom equality is believed to be one of the—if not the single—sovereign virtues. But within such a framework, Dworkin is honest enough to note further that, as a matter of principle, whenever a government's decisions 'keep the lives of poor people bleak [w]e must be prepared to explain, to those who suffer in that way, why they have nevertheless been treated with the equal concern that is their right' (2000, p 2).

This captures with subtlety the concern we can trace back through Tully's argument to the claim by Habermas that the 'normativity of the idea of equality itself' is not necessarily undermined by factual conditions of inequality. The point that I would like to make, however, by way of drawing together these reflections on politics and the economy, is that there is a suspicion that this idea itself *is* implicated, and is so because of the way it is given institutional vesting under contemporary social and economic conditions. The problem, in fact, is with the very *inclusive* nature of the claim to equality that the political ideal makes: hidden in it is the potential for modes of disaggregation that facilitate the separating out of stated ideals from responsibility for harms occurring. The clue to this can be found in the second quote from Dworkin and lies in the slippage between the 'we' and the 'they' in the claim he made: '*we* must be able to explain . . . why *they* have been treated with equal concern . . .' The disjunction here, quickly made then covered over ('*naturally*', said Habermas), paradoxically stems from a mode of inclusion that carries immense centripetal force: that is, arguments about an *idealised* equality *for all*. But such a homogenising logic, when actualised and put into practice under the kinds of property conditions and institutional forms we considered a moment ago, always sustains the disunity that—when it remains hidden, particularly through the invocation of an inclusive community of equal citizens—again *legitimates* wrongs that the sufferers find very hard to make heard.

Among the effects of this inclusive logic is a disaggregation of responsibility (or, in other terms, an organisation of irresponsibility) based on the postulated organisation of responsibility at a different level. That is, postulating a political community in the singular (conventionally, the 'We the people' of the nation state) as the responsible agent for that community works to *disavow* the experience of those who will not, or do not, seek to be so represented—those exploited, marginalised or discriminated against, for whom it makes no sense to be part of the inclusive 'we' of community ('we exploit ourselves'?), but who are nonetheless co-opted into it through a sense of community *as a whole*. These voices are therefore excluded through being included at another level, as *our* community: not 'this and this exploited or immiserated community', just 'our' community, the disjunction having vanished. As such, despite—even because of—the centripetal force of the postulated inclusive community, this way of thinking in fact works to *sever* relations of responsibility that may otherwise be attributable to specific, identifiable, structural, institutional and economic forms, and instead—

implausibly, partisanly—puts responsibility back on the community 'as a whole'. In this way, the logic of unity—proclaimed commonly through a single national constitutional narrative—and the actual asymmetries of the effects of governmental and economic power are removed from view and turned into something other than that which, in fact, they are.

Finally, it is worth noting that a variation of this occurs in the asymmetry to be found in the dominion exercised by a powerful government and its economic counterparts over citizens *outside* its jurisdiction. While, in the domestic sphere, the government tends to claim allegiance solely from its citizenry and claim dominion from those who come within its legal jurisdiction (as Dworkin noted), a particular government—its official institutional along with its unofficial adjunctival means of executing policy—*exercises* dominion and *secures* allegiance from people far beyond what it claims, or even could claim. The coincidence, for example, of US military and commercial power readily spreads throughout the globe in ways impossible to trap in terms even of conventional legitimatory discourses. Here, dominion is exercised in vastly asymmetrical ways that do not, even in theory, allow for the slightest measure of political accountability. And such conditions only multiply when we consider other key economic institutions and forms at which political supervision in the conventional sense is not even aimed, such as the IMF or WTO. For those who suffer the ravages of poverty or famine as their countries are forcefully integrated into the capital markets of WTO, World Bank and IMF-sponsored privatisation projects, all in the name of the 'self-regulating market', the asymmetries take on phenomenal, and brutal, proportions.

But even the legitimations offered by democratic theorists of equality work—*labour*—to hide this from too much exposure, with the kind of domestic and foreign policy consequences that are all too apparent. Hence why suffering consequent on these practices and ideals tends, in fact, *not* to show up as cognitive dissonances or crises. Immunised by the mechanisms of responsibility transference, underpinned by the naturalised economic realm of rights to private property upheld at almost any cost by state institutions, the irresponsible mentality appears not only as widely prevalent, but as legitimate. And such organised irresponsibility and legitimised immunities are called 'the law'.

The invisible hand of irresponsibility?

We now need to draw all of these strands together. Rather than summarise what has gone before, I would like to offer a metaphor that might stand as a way of thinking about the subject matter of this chapter. With our various references to the work of Adam Smith so far, it might be appropriate to refer to one of the more enduring of his images, even though it played a very minor role in his work: the 'invisible hand'. For Smith, each market actor pursued his own individual ends and, in so doing, 'neither intends to promote the publick interest, nor knows how much he is promoting it . . . he intends only his own gain, and he is in this, as in many other cases, led by an invisible hand to promote an end which was no part of his intention' (Smith, 1976, p 456). What stands out about invisible hand explanations, writes Ullmann-Margalit (1978), is that:

> . . . the phenomenon explained is shown to be the product neither of centralized decisions nor of explicit agreements to bring it about; rather, it is presented as the end result of a certain process that *aggregates the separate and 'innocent' actions of numerous dispersed individuals into an overall pattern* which is the very phenomenon we set out to account for.
>
> (Ullmann-Margalit, 1978, p 265, emphasis added)

In some respects, this image captures the phenomena I have been describing in this chapter: that the organisation of irresponsibility, the disappearance of responsibility and the proliferation of immunities among the practices of responsibility are neither the result of centralised decisions, nor of any actual consensus. There is no individual or collective intention through which responsibility is dispersed; rather, that occurs through a plurality of social forms, institutions, expectations and transferences. But while Smith's work saw this aspect as promoting good, the metaphor, we now see, might equally be applied to the production of harms. We drew on Bauman's work expressly in this regard, noting, with him, that highly organised and 'rational' social activities always have the potential to, and often do, deliver that which is 'inhuman and cruel in its consequences, *if not* its intention'.

But, in another respect, the temptation of this image needs to be avoided, because the very forms that provide the mechanisms of disavowal are never themselves 'aggregated into an overall pattern'. The invisible hand, here, does not do the work of bringing together that which was separate, but performs the contrary role: it is as if an invisible hand keeps *apart* all of these mechanisms so that, when seen from the *perspective of the experience of suffering*, there will be *no* aggregation possible—no aggregation that would reconnect that experience with its causes. Here *dis*aggregation is, and endures as, the norm.

Located in these same institutions that celebrate rationality, productivity, accountability, measurement, responsibility and wealth, the experience of extensive suffering appears—quite wrongly—as an excess, as irrational, as contradictory. But it is not. From the perspective of those who suffer, the 'hand' that causes suffering is seldom invisible. And neither is it here: it is the same one that celebrates rationality, productivity, accountability, and the rest.

Chapter 3

The laws of irresponsibility

Part I   Juridicial concepts and categories at work

The division of labour of legal responsibilities

What, and how, do law and legal institutions contribute to the organisation of irresponsibility? These are the questions that I will seek to answer in the course of this and the following chapter. This will involve investigating what is *specific* to the juridical realm in the contribution that it makes to the legitimation of human suffering. If it is the case that irresponsibility proliferates among practices of responsibility, as was argued in the previous chapter, then we would expect that law—as one of the most prominent social forms of organising responsibilities—will be deeply implicated in this. The purpose of what follows here, then, is to show how that expectation is, in fact, realised. In order to understand this fully, however, we need to pay attention not only to what constitutes the distinctiveness of juridical forms and institutions, but also to keep in mind that these forms and institutions variously draw on, augment or supplement the broader social forms we have just analysed.

There are a variety of facets to this analysis that need to be covered. But let us begin by looking at something that follows directly from two important elements of the insights gained in the previous chapter: namely, role responsibility in the context of the division of labour. Legal norms and institutions contribute to these in an important sense. In the first place, legal categories define forms of acting that simply *are* constitutive of role responsibilities. The number of such legal roles is enormous and familiar: tenant; landlord; employee; employer; taxpayer; citizen; and so on. Some legal roles exist as legal creations even though they may play other functions too. For example, citizenship is a legal category, but one that has important political aspects; tenant and landlord are also usually legally defined roles, although they play important economic and, to an extent, political functions. Some legal categories fasten onto existing roles and relationships, but come to define them partly in legal terms: for example, the relationship between parent and child brings with it today significant legal rights and obligations. Other legal categories might best be thought of as being more akin to defining a legal status, rather than a role as such: for example, the rights and duties attaching to legal persons for liability in delict or in contractual relations might be understood to define legal roles, although they will not always be experienced as such. Finally, legal roles need not attach to living persons at all but to legal creations, such as corporations or forms of government, the roles of which may involve, for example, the rights and obligations that come with being property holders or pertaining to defined offices, among many others.

When we think about legal categories in the sense of providing statuses and roles, we come to see that law is replete with role responsibilities. But what is immediately interesting about these is the way in which one of their key purposes is precisely to *circumscribe* the range of rights and obligations that attach to the role. So, for example, the contractor or mortgage holder will have certain enumerated legal rights and duties—many of which, such as price or repayment schedules, will be made by agreement—that set out the range and limits of liabilities. These are likely to be supplemented by further conditions that are imposed upon the parties through statute or common law, such as duties to bargain in good faith or to avoid forms of misrepresentation. Likewise, a local authority will have a range of powers delegated to it in its governmental role, powers that will be supervised by administrative laws specific to the nature of the institution, as well as by the generally applicable rules of private and criminal law, etc. Across the range of legal activities, then, roles are defined in ways that both create and limit liabilities. They do so, moreover—and we will return to this aspect later—in a way that normally allows not only for clarification of, but, in cases of dispute, for resolution of the content and scope of these responsibilities through the intervention of third parties who are empowered to adjudicate, such as courts. Features of this kind are commonly seen as a distinctive achievement of legal norms and institutions, in that they offer certainty and predictability across relations and over time.

Now, in the context of the observations made in the previous chapter, we can note that this kind of legal ordering replicates features of the division of labour that are of more widespread social significance. Legal categories might be thought to contribute to this in a dual sense. Firstly, within the realm of legal regulation, legal rights and duties attaching to particular roles are ways of dividing up the juridical field itself (to use Pierre Bourdieu's (1987) phrase). This field is not only constituted by way of jurisdiction at a general level (the jurisdiction of a state or of an international order, say), but is itself made up of a plethora of smaller jurisdictions pertaining to all manner of legal roles, from courts and legislatures, to corporations and clubs. In this sense, there is a division of legal labour according to which particular activities are divided up in more or less clearly defined terms. Here, in other words, legal roles work to demarcate the boundaries of responsibilities in ways that are facilitated by the division of competencies, rights and obligations. Moreover, within any particular legally regulated activity, there is likely, in fact, to be a range of different legal responsibilities attaching to it: for example, the activities of a solicitor or medical doctor will be subject to laws relating to duties to clients or patients, to standards of professional conduct and misconduct, as well as to criminal and fiscal liabilities. With regard to each of these, the standards and duties may vary according to the particular legal area involved and there will usually be further divisions of legal responsibility that correspond to organisational hierarchies within particular practices.

To recall an earlier observation, it is important to note that, in all of these senses, the division of legal labour is not well understood as a fragmentation of responsibilities, at least if that is to be understood in a temporal sense: they are not fragments of a once-greater whole because they never were 'whole' or capable of being understood in a singular way in the first place. Nor are they best thought of as each referring back to some singular or platonic notion of 'pure' responsibility, of which they are merely instances or paler copies. Rather, in the way in which we described role responsibilities more generally, they are each 'normative devices' that correspond to particular needs, expectations and interests, and are instantiations of *these* dynamics, not some greater or singular notion of responsibility. We will come back to this point again in a later section.

The second contribution that legal role responsibilities can be seen to offer is in terms of the demarcations that legal categories can effect in respect of non-legal modes of organisation. Seen in broader social terms, legal roles form one part of the division of labour of responsibility practices across a whole range of normative forms and relationships: for example, political or moral responsibility practices may be understood to be distinguishable from, and operate on different terms to, legal responsibilities. In most instances, certain aspects of these normative forms or relationships may be subject to legal regulation, while others may not be: in the case of the parent–child relationship, for example, legal involvement only pertains to certain kinds of activities and does not, of course, define entirely the roles of parent and child. What involvement there is for legal norms, how it 'intervenes', and where the boundary is to be drawn between these and other responsibility practices will be historically contingent and will vary according to a number of factors. But that there are such *boundaries* to be observed is a function of the different modes of cognition and action that are specific to *legal* categories.

One key feature of the distinctiveness of these categories, indeed of the juridical realm generally, is very obvious, but no less significant for being so. There is an ability—in fact, a *duty*—to refer to sources of legal authority as embodied in a range of legal texts, including constitutions, custom, statutes, case reports, etc. As Neil MacCormick (1995, p 469) puts it, 'legal argumentation can never proceed acceptably without some basis in some argument from authority'. Such 'authority reasons' are supplemented, he observes, by 'substantive reasons'—such as general principles, values and standards—that play a role in making 'intelligible (not to say acceptable) any claim of authority', but these substantive reasons will, however, be limited to the range of reasons authorised within the legal institutional realm. Legal norms and structures thus employ both authority and substantive reasons in order to establish an overall and specific rationality to legal norms within an institutional setting, in ways that allow them to be distinguished from other normative forms or institutions. The consequence of this is important because it means that:

> The special sort of [juridical] reasoning is one which leaves aside any general and abstract deliberation on what in a given context it would be best or would be all things considered right to do or not do. Where law is appealed to, all things are not considered. Rather, the law's requirements (and, perhaps, enablements and permissions) are considered, and decision focuses on application of, or compliance with these requirements (etc), or 'norms' more generally.
>
> (MacCormick, 1995, p 469)

That *all things are not considered* is one key aspect for understanding how law can be understood to provide boundaries between alternative normative readings of relationships. In doing so, legal regulation, in its reliance on specific authoritative, interpretative and classificatory techniques, provides a form of legitimacy that is not straightforwardly reducible to the direct expression of interest or preference—a legitimacy that lies precisely in requiring distinctive *forms* of reasoning in the context of institutionalised authoritative norms. Drawing on what is referred to as the 'power of form', for Bourdieu (1987), the juridical field comprises processes of systematisation, formalisation, rationalisation and universalisation, which play a vital role in asserting and maintaining the distinctiveness and legitimacy of the force of law. As such, argues Bourdieu:

> Far from being a simple ideological mask, such rhetoric of autonomy, neutrality, and universality . . . is the expression of the whole operation of the juridical field and, in particular, of the work of rationalization to which the system of juridical norms is continually subordinated.
>
> (Bourdieu, 1987, p 820)

Now all of this is, I think, largely uncontroversial. But we should note right away an implication of this: given the way in which legal roles function to *limit* responsibilities attaching to them, and do so in reasonably clear and authoritative terms, we can see that they provide ways of both asserting *and* denying responsibilities. This can occur in respect of each of the two senses that we have just noted: namely, it can occur internally to the juridical field itself and in its relation to other forms of social practice. That it does so, and how it does so, links directly to the role of law in organising irresponsibility in the context of the more widespread asymmetry between suffering and establishing responsibility for it. So let us now take note of some further features of this by way of a few examples, before turning to examine their conceptual underpinnings.

Consider, firstly, that legal role responsibilities divide up legal activities in ways that allow for responsibility not to be transferred across to different parts of the juridical field. For example, what would ordinarily constitute an assault in criminal law—deliberate infliction of physical harm—will not register *as* criminal in certain other legally authorised circumstances, even though the physical act is the same: if the harm is carried out in a boxing match or by a surgeon making a scalpel incision, for example. On another level, the pursuit of activities under the authority of state sovereignty will disallow legal responsibilities that may otherwise have been relevant. For example, if a state deploys extensive, although legally authorised military violence, it will not be liable for breaches of human rights on civilian populations if the violations are the result of actions that are proportionate to military ends and if there is no deliberate intention to target civilians. This is so even though such human rights violations are entirely foreseeable when massive force is unleashed. In cases such as these, the assertion of legal rights in the context of certain defined roles or activities simultaneously carries with it corresponding immunities, even for those activities that cause widespread harms and abuses of legal rights. Furthermore, and again in line with some observations made in the previous chapter, legal categories can be used to separate out or distance responsibility connections temporally. That is, legal mechanisms, such as statutes of limitation and rules about prescription, divide up and compartmentalise responsibilities temporally by limiting the reach of legal responsibilities over time through the introduction of cut-off dates, time-barred actions and the like. These may be put to use across a range of social activities and harms, for example, to block claims about criminal responsibilities in cases where crimes are deemed to have 'gone stale' by the passing of time, or to negate restitutive claims for reparations for historic injustices, and so on.

These processes of compartmentalisation can also be discerned in respect of the second sense, in which the legal role legitimately disallows the transference of responsibilities for harms from the legal realm to those that are non-legal. Consider the following scenarios. A business acting within its legal powers will not be held responsible for activities that are deliberately aimed at harming the economic well-being of other businesses: for example, opening a music store next to an existing one is likely to harm the latter's business, but the legality of the competitive activity nullifies any responsibility for that harm. Similarly, the legal rights of a shareholder in a corporation will not be deemed to make him or her responsible for the outcomes of the management decisions of the corporation, nor for activities that the corporation carries out that cause extensive, although legally authorised, harms such as deforestation, sweatshop labour, etc. Or at an international level, thinking back to the example in Chapter 1, the legal role of the state in pursuing sanctions might be deemed sufficient to negate claims about political or moral responsibility for the devastating effects of the sanctions regime. Legal role responsibilities can thus be seen as providing ways in which legal actors can understand and use that role to nullify or distance themselves from the causing of harms. In these ways, we can see again how legal categories might involve both internal and external aspects of the division of labour of responsibilities and, we should add, that this might also have a 'vertical' dimension, whereby responsibilities are deemed not transferable up (or down) organisational hierarchies.

If some of these examples appear to be truisms, there is nonetheless something important going on here, because what is conspicuous about them is the way in which questions are, or can be, raised about how far beyond each particular legal category or role the influence of the specific rights or obligations extend. For example, is it really the case that the shareholder is in no way implicated in the manner in which the corporation causes harms, given that he or she *benefits* economically, in the form of dividends, from these self-same activities? Is it the case that beneficiaries who live in states that have perpetrated historical injustices have no responsibilities at all to victims or their descendants when it comes to claims for reparation? Are citizens in no sense responsible for the harmful acts of their governments, when these acts are paid for by the citizens' taxes and they democratically elect the government? In each of these cases, we see that contestation may emerge around the boundaries regarding the legitimacy of the limitations (or otherwise) of legal roles, in ascertaining the extent to which further imputations of responsibility may extend. This is reinforced by the fact that some of these examples are of much contemporary relevance and dispute—indeed, I explicitly take up the final question in the last chapter.

How should we understand the significance of this? Let us note three points. The first is rather obvious, but still needs stating—that the legal boundary that delimits responsibility is never finally or naturally fixed, but is contingent. Secondly, even though we acknowledge this contingency, it is nevertheless the case that, if the boundary *is* instantiated, it can, and often does, play a strong role in (legitimately) blocking off or immunising challenges from other normative sources or claims. To understand this, we can refer back to the observations made at the end of Chapter 1 concerning the three aspects of the juridical architecture. There, it will be recalled, we emphasised how law's claim to correctness, its force and its social priority were central to law's role under contemporary social conditions. Here, we return to these aspects by noting that they—and, in this context, it is particularly law's force and social priority—provide a legitimating mechanism for trumping alternative or competing normative claims when it comes to understanding the impact of legal role responsibility.

Consider again the example of the shareholder. It is possible that the shareholder—or a group of shareholders—may come under criticism for the corporation's investment in a particular activity that is alleged to be harmful to others or to the environment. But the legality of the role of shareholder means that he or she is under no obligation to respond to that charge. The legal understanding carries a far greater force. As Paddy Ireland (2003) notes, in a discussion of the historical emergence of the contemporary form of shares and shareholding, this immunity became generic in nature in the nineteenth century, when 'the rise of the fully paid-up share and the resulting elimination of residual shareholder liabilities [meant] that joint stock company shares became completely *unencumbered rights to revenue to which no responsibilities or obligations attached*' (Ireland, 2003, p 257, emphasis added). Underpinned, in this instance, by a particular legal form and given social priority by legal enforcement, the legal role responsibility of the shareholder was safely removed from the matter of responding to critical claims. Moreover, and possibly even more significantly because it compounds this legal understanding, the reality of shareholding lends itself to an even greater compartmentalisation through the complexity of legal relations, which may involve a further set of distancing techniques when the shareholder is itself merely an intermediary between intended beneficiary and ultimate harm. The case of contributors to a pension scheme provides a good example of this. The financial contribution is mediated through contribution mechanisms, pension funds, investment fund managers, diversified portfolios, etc., in such a way that not only is the contributor distanced from the alleged harm, but he or she usually has very little idea how and where the contribution is being invested, far less a sensitivity to criticism on the grounds of *his or her own* alleged role in producing harm. This is not to say that 'ethical investment' cannot be demanded or promoted. But, at least as it is conventionally understood or at least as it is conventionally acted upon, this has very little bearing on the experience, such as it is, of the pension contributor. Moreover and more decisively, and we will see more clearly why in a moment, any such 'ethics' are already of an extremely circumscribed nature: they involve only variations on the theme of how properly to make profits in a capitalist market.

We should, however, add this caveat: just as we saw in the previous chapter that distances in time and space are not absolute, but fixed to particular stakes, so too does the legal mechanism here allow distance *and* proximity to operate simultaneously. In the case of the pension fund, the contribution is expected to make a *direct economic* return to the contributor: *that* is not distanced. Contributors expect a return and, if that is put at risk, the immediacy of the relation between the ultimate economic activity and risk of gain and loss *is* understood as perfectly proximate, even though the manner of its attainment and any effects in terms of possible harms is easily distanced. One can readily think of many such situations whereby economic returns are prioritised and yet their potentially detrimental effects on others or the environment are compartmentalised, and understood, if indeed they are grasped at all, as distant.

Here, in other words, we are dealing with something that is reminiscent of a two-way mirror: what is blocked from one perspective is perfectly passable or transparent from the other. The invocation of a particular legal category—share, legal right, corporation—contributes an important means of allowing benefits to be legitimately expected in one direction, while disbenefits or harms to others are blocked and thus fail to register as a matter of, or for, responsibility. This gives further credence to the argument that responsibilities—in this instance, legal role responsibilities—are best understood as normative devices, the technology of which may be used to promote not responsibility *per se* (whatever that might mean), but responsibility practices geared to the promotion of particular goals, interests and expectations. But it matters that the promotion of these goals, interests, etc. is mediated through the legal form: the specificity of that form offers a distinctive mode of operation that compartmentalises responsibilities and provides a legitimacy for activities that are decidedly asymmetrical in their make-up and consequences. The 'legal technology' of responsibility, in other words, provides an expert means for connecting benefits and disconnecting harms within the same activity, and it does so in a legally objective, coercive and socially effective manner. It ensures that all things are not considered

This leads to the third point, which, although it follows from the previous one, is often less apparent. Legal norms and actions operating within the legal realm are to be understood as not only contributing to establishing the boundary between the legal and non-legal realms themselves, but also as influencing what lies *beyond* the boundary. While legal roles play a necessary part in understanding, situating and challenging where the boundaries are to be drawn, and while they offer mechanisms of blockage and passage along the lines we have just noted, it is also the case that they necessarily *also* influence what is deemed to be the *other* side of the boundary. That is, where legal categories are involved in the division of labour of responsibility, they inevitably have influence beyond the ostensible sphere of their own regulatory activity; they influence, more or less directly and observably, the way in which *other* normative sources come to be constituted or acted upon. This does not happen uniformly or with the same intensity across different activities—but it is vital to acknowledge that it *does* happen, particularly given the increasingly prominent role of law and legal mechanisms in contemporary society.

One way of thinking about this is to note the conditions of juridification to which we drew attention at the end of Chapter 1. Here, it will be remembered, processes that saw the spread and intensification of legal norms in society meant that these norms came to play an increasing role in organising normative forms and hierarchies generally. As Habermas (1996) forcefully described it, it was more and more the case that law became 'the only medium in which it is possible reliably to establish morally obligated relationships of mutual respect even amongst strangers'.

But the point here is slightly different from that: while there are undoubtedly variations in intensity across the range of legal regulatory activity, it is in no way an exaggeration to say that there is barely a realm of social interaction that is not in some way touched by the juridical realm. Often this is so deeply ingrained, so naturalised, that it fails to register at all. While there are processes of juridification taking place, the legally constituted forms we have in mind here are concerned less with the expansion of formal law into previously legally unregulated areas, but more with some of the most elementary organisational features of modern society. Let me give a couple of examples by way of illustration.

Drawing on part of the analysis at the end of the last chapter, we should pay attention to the primary economic role of property laws, which institute regulatory forms relating to the ownership and exchange of private property rights. Such laws have a bearing not only on activities such as commercial transactions, but also profoundly affect a whole range of practices, the essence of which is nonetheless reducible neither to legal nor to economic determination as such. To borrow Foucault's formulation: 'to govern' generally means to 'structure the field of action of others' (Foucault, 1983, p 221). Thus, property law and rights, for example, inevitably affect family and domestic relations as well as educational and health practices. They affect the ways in which these relations and practices are, although only partly, set limits in respect of how their own ideals and goals are to be achieved or reproduced. But these effects and limits are no less powerful because the influence of the legal categories of property law may not directly organise them (although, in certain cases, they may); rather, they are powerful because these legal categories form the ground rules according to which these practices must be played out. The reality and impact of these influences only occasionally tend to become more obvious, but even then tend quickly to be naturalised: for example, as has been happening recently, where there is an intensification of the commodification of public goods and social activities occurring generally in the context of privatisation policies and programmes. Here, public goods and social relations do not themselves have to be juridified as such for them nonetheless to be profoundly influenced by the wider structuring of the juridical field and the deployment of existing categories of property rights within it.

We find similar structural effects in respect of public or constitutional laws. These laws, which often seem distant from day-to-day social life, are, of course, crucial elements in respect of the conditions that they set for social relations through such legal definitions of the status of the 'right to rights' within any given jurisdiction. Here, again, the usually taken-for-granted importance of these becomes more visible when that right is contested, as has been the case recently regarding asylum seekers or migrants. But the way in which legal categories have come to influence political debate on such matters—they do not, of course, completely determine them—should not be overlooked. So, in respect of public law, when Martin Loughlin (2000, ch 13) writes about an increasing 'legalization of politics' in what he calls our 'age of rights', we can understand by this both that political conflicts can be seen increasingly as being translated into legal terms (for example, where political disputes are no longer simply a matter of disputes over policy, but come to be framed in terms of disputes over competing rights claims that can be adjudicated by courts); and we also understand that this process witnesses, in turn, a partial transformation in the nature of *politics* as a consequence of the insertion into the realm of political conflict a mode of dealing with that conflict, which now comes to be understood in *justiciable* terms.

What underpin these developments generally, then, are fundamental conditions of legal intervention that facilitate the reduction of complex conflicts into those that are commensurable and therefore resolvable. This mode of understanding and action, this demand *of* law, can be seen, in turn, as providing one of the demands *for* law: the legal form is seen to be desirable not because of its substantive rationality, but because of the value of its instrumental deployment—the difference it can effect on the reality as a means of providing authoritative verdicts.

In precisely these ways, we can begin to understand how non-legal activities are influenced, more or less directly and successfully, by the active presence of the legal form *even if* these activities are not wholly, or even explicitly, juridified. The shift in expectations and presentation that comes with the presence of legal rights and third-party decidability—as well as the particular legal categories themselves, which structure the intervention of law—affects how the original normative practice or conflicts arising from it are understood. These changes are attested to, perhaps most emphatically, by the fact that, where legal institutions and norms have indeed achieved social predominance, other forms of normative claim that seek authentication, recognition or approval tend increasingly to be required to be made by reference to the framework of *legal* regulation, and thus to be expressed in terms that conform to the specific modes of legal cognition, reasoning and decision making. It is the difference that legal norms and the structure of litigation within an institutionalised coercive setting make that may, in turn, see the legally authorised recognition of a claim become a prize to be sought. It is worth having, because it has a legitimacy, it has social priority and it brings with it the ability to be enforced: such is the power of the specific form of law under contemporary social conditions, and its influence extends beyond the reach of its formally authorised boundaries. As Bourdieu noted:

> These performative [legal] utterances—substantive as opposed to procedural—decisions publicly formulated by authorized agents acting on behalf of the collectivity, are magical acts which succeed because they

have the power to make themselves universally recognized. They thus
succeed in creating a situation in which no one can refuse or ignore the
power of view, the vision, which they impose.

(Bourdieu, 1987, p 838)

Now, for our purposes, the point about both the private and public law
examples is that legal categories can, and do, structure social relations at such
deep levels that questions of responsibility and irresponsibility tend already
to be underpinned or influenced by forms of law and legal role responsibilities that necessarily serve to limit the potential as to what, and how, alternative normative understandings may appear. These observations, therefore,
serve to supplement the idea that we explored in the previous chapter concerning the way in which claims about the priority of moral responsibility
untouched by social structures is implausible. In this instance, we can now see
how the juridical realm and its modes of regulation and role definition can be
understood as making their own distinctive contribution to general features
of social organisation, and to the nature and experience of social relations.
Basic conceptions of public and private law thus fundamentally structure
what appear as 'natural' or given characteristics of social life in very specific
ways, and it is this that gives them their potential to overdetermine non-legal
normative ideas and responses and to do so in much the same way as that
which led us earlier to reject notions about the purity or priority of moral
responsibility.

That said, there is often a train of argument that would urge us to see the
increased influence and invocation of legal norms in wider economic or political discourse as being a way of 'responsibilising' these activities that, previously, have been left to the arbitrary whim of economic or political forces and
policies. But such a conclusion is unpersuasive. On the one hand, the emergence of an increasingly litigious society does not, despite temptations to
understand it otherwise, amount to a more generally 'responsible' society if
we mean this in the sense of it being more attuned to the suffering of others,
or of it being a more solidaristic society. The most obvious reason why not is
that this reading gets cause and effect the wrong way round: rather than
confirming a general society-wide impetus to create a more responsible society—for which law would become the expression—legal responsibilisation is,
arguably, a signal of, and a way of dealing with, the *breakdown* of alternative
forms of responsibility practices. Thus it is this *deficit* that is marked by the
increasing resort to legal forms, precisely because of the inability of these
alternative practices to deal adequately with conflicts arising over responsibilities. But that does not mean that legal responsibilisation can make good
that deficit—or at least, it can only do so according to its reformation in legal
terms. Such 'legal solidarity' represents a solidarity of a very distinctive
type, that is, a highly emaciated solidarity corresponding in its modern form
to the 'society of strangers'; a solidarity, in other words, that is based on a

calculative, or calculating, measure, the form of which is essentially that of competing rights claims and their adjudication. In this sense, legal responsibilisation is as much a marker of a decline in interpersonal trust, since there is ordinarily very little co-ordinated, imaginative or communal potential when it comes to litigation or the shadow it casts.

On the other hand, in so far as legal categories define and compartmentalise responsibilities into discrete role responsibilities, they have *at one and the same time* the potential to inscribe alternative forms of denials of responsibility. This can occur in both aspects to which we have drawn attention: both internally to the legal field and in respect of its relations with non-legal practices. In a myriad of ways, legal norms are just as capable of distancing responsibility for harms or of transferring understanding of these harms across practices in ways that lead to the legitimation or disappearance of those harms. As we saw, for example, with the case of the shareholder, the introduction of complexes of legal norms makes it easier to distance beneficiaries from the impacts of the profit-making activity. In this respect, the influence or intervention of the categories offered by the legal field, when combined with law's force and claim to correctness, should make us wary of the nature of 'responsibility' that law brings; it is just as likely to entrench the operation of irresponsibility practices.

Despite these observations, we should nevertheless also avoid a temptation of seeing legal norms as entirely dominating the field of responsibility practices. Often, certain legal standards will be legitimately overridden by further policy considerations and nowhere is this clearer than in the example of the violations of human rights that can be carried out in the name of protecting state sovereignty or security. But even then, these latter policy goals are themselves most powerful when they are legitimated *legally*—in other words, when human rights violations are carried out in the name of the law.

It is for these reasons, then, that we need to be highly suspicious of any claim that the intervention of legal norms leads to heightened standards of responsibility for legal or other actors. The invocation of legal roles and responsibilities may track and embolden the pursuit of policies, the consequence, if not intention, of which is the disappearance of responsibility for harms caused. In this sense, the division of labour of legal responsibilities needs to be situated within a context of what we might refer to as 'structural complicities' between different social systems, which, according to the image of the two-way mirror, foster relations of simultaneous connection and disconnection that can operate at once to facilitate and legitimise the production of harms under conditions that will be deemed to be perfectly normal.

Damage without injury

If these observations build upon sociological reference points, then there is another powerful sense in which legal forms of responsibility produce simultaneous immunities from responsibility and it is one that can be initi-ated in respect of an understanding of the operation of the legal norm itself. That is, there is a *conceptual* reading of legal normativity that sees it as an elementary means of producing irresponsibility in its more profound sense, as the 'disappearing' of responsibility for harms. This reading of legal action to which we must now turn is one that concerns *neither* a claim about the dam-aging consequences of such action, nor a claim that the substantive content of the legal norm is 'bad' or unwise and hence irresponsible in that sense; rather, it inheres in the conception of legal normativity itself. In order to explore this, we can trace its appearance in the work of two seminal thinkers in the modern tradition.

Thomas Hobbes (1991, p 137) argued that 'the word *injustice* relates to some law; *injury* to some person, as well as some law'. This formulation might be thought to have an obvious etymological derivation—injury as *in-juria*—but it involves more than that, because it brings to the fore a crucial distinc-tion between injury and *damage*. Damage, says Hobbes, is some harm that is suffered by a person, which is not an injury because it breaches no law. Hobbes gives two examples: where a servant is commanded by his master to convey a sum of money to a third party and the servant fails to carry this out, the servant has damaged the third party, but injured only his master because he was under an obligation only to the master and not to the third party. Analogously, although on a bigger scale, where a person causes harm to someone who is beyond the bounds of the contractually established civil government, then that 'evil' will not register as an injury because the sufferer is not party to the laws of the government.

This is a decisive distinction and it is one that exemplifies one of the func-tions of legal role responsibility of which we took note above: that if 'dam-age' (in Hobbes' sense) results, then only that which is in breach of the law allows it to register as a matter of injury or injustice. For those whose suffer-ing is beyond the legal relation, there can be damage, but no injustice. But this point has an important corollary that is less often given emphasis. What is so significant about this way of formulating the issue is that, if legal standards define injustice, then it is also the case that law defines *damage* too: if law can recognise some damages as injuries—if law sets some standard or test for ascertaining which damages will count as injuries—then the law also defines, by exclusion, that which will count as damage, but not injury. Such suffering is, legally speaking, legitimate.

But this is only part of the story, and Hobbes supplements this observation with a distinction between just *actions* and a just *person*. Just actions are actions that signify 'what is done with right', while unjust actions are those that are done with injury. This is a different matter from the justness or unjustness of a person, which refers to his or her inclination to do justice or to neglect it. Therefore 'he who hath done some just thing is not therefore said to be a *just* Person, but *guiltlesse* and he that hath done some unjust thing, we doe not therefore say he is an *unjust,* but *guilty* man' (Hobbes, 1991, p 138, emphasis in original). Conformity with a law, *conformity to the legal obliga-tion,* makes the legal actor—and the language is significant here—*guiltless*; that is, according to this understanding, there is justification for the belief that responsible actions—just actions, responsible actions according to the law—cannot simultaneously be injurious or irresponsible.

To bring the two points together, we can note this: suffering that is not illegal because it is beyond the bounds of the legal norms is thus legitimated; and suffering caused by acting on the basis of legal norms is likewise legitim-ate. Since actions in fulfillment of the legal norm make the actor guiltless.

In slightly different terms, Kant (1991, pp 50, 53) makes a similar point according to which we have a confirmation of the same powerful logic: 'A deed is *right* or *wrong* in general . . . insofar as it conforms with duty or is contrary to it.' In fact, he adds, 'conduct in keeping with what is owed has no rightful effect at all'. Hence, for Kant, the matter of responsibility stops there—with the obligation—and cannot be taken further to refer to, or con-flict with, contradictory normative considerations *or* the harmful outcomes of legal acts. As he argues: 'The good or bad *results* of an action that is owed, like the results of omitting a meritorious action, cannot be imputed to the subject.' Put in individualist terms, the implication is that 'I am not respon-sible for anything as long as I do not, in the narrowly defined circumstances of my personal interaction, commit a wrong' (Bankowski, 2001, p 35); I am, as Hobbes put it, guiltless.

From these points, we come to understand that legal norms set the terms according to which damage does or does not amount to injury and, further-more, that this has implications for the legal actor, in that he or she is not responsible for legal actions that cause damage—because they cause no injury—since suffering which is beyond the scope of law, does not register as a matter of, or for, legal responsibility. According to this analysis, then, legal actions that produce suffering produce, at one and the same time, an impun-ity for the legal actor vis à vis that suffering. Only unjust actions, actions in *breach* of the law, can cause injury—'*in-juria*'—and this may result in a sanc-tion or punishment for the actor; just actions, by contrast—that is, actions in conformity with the law—that produce suffering are, necessarily, free from punishment ('*in-poena*': impunity).

One way of thinking about this is to see that it fleshes out the claim to cor-rectness—the claim to justice intrinsic to law that results from the 'structure of legal acts and legal reasoning' (Alexy, 2004, p 164). What we now see is that, like the soldier 'obeying orders', the legal actor's responsibility is trans-ferred to the legal norm itself, which stands as authority for negating his or her responsibility since it makes him or her guiltless. Responsibility stops with the fulfilment of the legal obligation—and that is an end to the matter. There is, in other words, a compartmentalisation that is a function of legal categorisation: the legal actor (who may be an individual, a corporation or a judge) is merely the *conduit* of legal authority and this is so—perhaps importantly so—even if the actor has discretion in how to interpret the law or how to carry out the legal role. The judge, for example, is usually understood not to be *personally* responsible for the legal judgment he or she pronounces: rather it is the state of the law that is responsible for the legal judgment pronounced: 'the law', not the judge's personal opinion, is declared in the decision and it is the decision's *legal* reasoning that must do the work of justifying the outcome, not the reasoning of the actual person. That person is merely, even when he or she has discretion, the agent or mouthpiece of the law and his or her personal views are, legally speaking, irrelevant. In these senses, the judge is not responsible because legal responsibility in accordance with the law and the legal role *is* non-responsibility for the person. This is legal responsibility's vanishing point.

But if so, then there is one further consequence that cannot be avoided and it links back to the nature of role responsibility: if these conditions hold, then because responsible action is action in obedience to the duly constituted legal authority and because '*I am not responsible*' for rightful action, it turns out that 'Our autonomy vanishes' (Bankowski, 2001, p 40). In this sense, the legal category provides the measure for, and the denial of, responsibilities. Hence, the person fulfilling the legal role is a means, not an end, for a legitimation that occurs elsewhere. Legal justification attaches only to legal norms and roles, and is not a matter for the person who happens to be in that role. This is best seen as an instantiation of an earlier general observation: for the autonomy of the *person* fulfilling the role to be genuine, that person would have to be able justifiably to exceed the role; he or she would have to be able to refuse to follow its dictates. The person who is a judge, of course, *might* do this: but if he or she were to do so, then he or she would no longer be a judge. So long as that person remains a judge, personal autonomy vanishes.

It is important to recognise just how profound an implication this has. What it shows is that the legal role overdetermines the content, and even appearance, of alternative normative ideals or claims, including moral or personal ones, because the role usurps the autonomy of the person who fills the role. When it comes to human beings acting in legal roles, there is only *one* living person who can act; if the law determines that a particular action is the right action, it cannot also be right *not* so to act for that person. There is only one actor and one possible action when it comes to either obeying or disobeying the law. If the actor obeys the law, he or she is guiltless; if he or she disobeys, the person is not. The one person cannot be both—guilty and guiltless—and certainly the action cannot be both, in respect of its effects. At the extreme point, as Detmold (1984) has argued, a judge, for example, who must legally sentence someone to death cannot plausibly say it is legally correct but morally wrong to authorise carrying out the judicial execution: if it is morally wrong to kill, it cannot be morally right to kill, even though it is authorised by the law. The person will be executed or will not be executed. The judge's claim to reserve his or her moral judgment is neither here nor there to that person condemned to death, nor does it have any independent force (other than some kind of self-serving consolation). The reason for this is that, if to fulfil the *legal* role means carrying through the execution and the judge goes through with this, then the legal role will also determine the morality of the act.

This example may sound extreme, but it is not; it is, in fact, the normal operation of action according to legal authority. (Even the example of judicial authorisation of killing is something that appears quite frequently in medical law cases, for example, when withdrawal of life support is authorised by judges.) One of the most profound expressions of this that I have come across was in the words of a South African judge, who made a submission to the Truth and Reconciliation Commission in the following terms:

> If lawyers and Judges were complicit under apartheid in enforcing injustice and inequity, they have no less responsibility for doing so under the present system . . . [W]e live in a [democratic] society still distinguished by extremes of dispossession. As a judge . . . I am nevertheless party to the injustices that still exist in our society; and my role in the enforcement of a system that contains injustices necessarily makes me complicit in them.
>
> (Edwin Cameron, quoted in Dyzenhaus, 1998, p 174)

But does this not contradict the claim made a moment ago that the judge is 'not personally responsible for the legal judgment' he or she gives? The answer lies in the fact that the law's claim to correctness, in accordance with which the person fulfilling the legal role acts, overrides any other question about that person's responsibility. He or she is under no obligation to respond in any other way to criticisms that may be made of his or her judgments. The person's response—his or her 'response-ability', to put it rather awkwardly—is limited to the *legal* justification. We would not say that judges are *personally* responsible for the justice of the decisions and consequences of all of the cases they make; likewise, they are not responsible for all the inequalities they render. The judge may, like Cameron, acknowledge some sense of complicity in reproducing an unequal society—but, just as likely, they may not. And this is the key point: the fact that it does not matter. That individual's personal responsibility, even his or her personal *autonomy*, is irrelevant so long as he or she remains a judge. In this sense, such people become, as Milgram (1974) suggested, no longer the efficient cause of *their own* actions; their duty—in the case of judges, because of their oath—is to uphold the law, not to do what they personally think right. And as we have seen, action in conformity with an obligation has 'no rightful effect'. Yet if this is correct, it is also one of the key reasons why it is *so* difficult to see such obligatory behaviour *as* wrong.

Of course, there remains one possible objection to this: the person may be tempted to see his or her autonomy *as* being fulfilled by willingly carrying out the role. This would be similar to the social contract idea that it is through obedience to rules of which one is the author that one can be free. But, in this context, trying to assert that idea would make two mistakes: firstly, it would fail to see that role responsibilities do not operate like this mode of justification, because actors do not define roles, but rather *vice versa*; secondly, it would conflate self-identification in the role with the institutional, justificatory and coercive means employed by the law. But these cannot be a matter for, or of, personal autonomy unless it is in terms of a breathtaking self-conceit or vanity: that '*le rôle, c'est moi*'!

Conceptually, then, this aspect of the form of legal thought and practice is—to use a metaphor made popular by Ronald Dworkin (1977)—like a trump card: it trumps any other claim about responsibility even when the legal action results in harm or extensive suffering. (This is another manifestation of MacCormick's observation (1995) that in law 'not all things are considered', only the demands of the law that necessarily fall to be considered.) Such suffering may be 'damage' but it is not injury, and in following the legal norm or role, the legal actor has an impunity in respect of such damage.

Hence, there is one final implication of this mode of thought: the full significance and power of it is that certain harms are impossible to register *as* harms because they are definitionally incapable of being understood as 'injuries'. This is akin to what Valerie Kerruish has called the '*wrong of law*' (see Kerruish, 1998, for whom this notion is worked through in the logical and epistemological frameworks of modern Western thought). This refers not to a criticism of the substance of law, of its moral or political fairness or otherwise, but rather to the wrong *of* law. In terms I have been using here, it is concerned with the fact that the law cannot be *both* right (correct or just) *and* wrong (unjust), and the wrong of law inheres precisely in this: harms cannot register because law's claim to correctness cannot be, at one and the same time, law's injustice. The 'wrong' of law is thus to be understood in a double sense: the experience of suffering consequent on legal action, but the removal of the very possibility of demonstrating that the infliction of harm has occurred—*because* it is the result of legal action. Jean-Francois Lyotard (1988, p 7) captured this well when he distinguished between a damage and a *wrong*, whereby 'a wrong would be a damage accompanied by the *loss of the means to prove the damage*' (emphasis added). It is this 'double silencing' (Christodoulidis and Veitch, 1997) that constitutes the more profound sense of irresponsibility that we have been considering here: it constitutes the disappearance of the *possibility* of responsibility.

This might sound—it does sound—highly abstract. It would remain so were it not for the fact that it is precisely this logic that lies at the root of the how law contributes to the *legitimacy* of extensive suffering under 'normal' legal conditions. Again, to re-emphasise, we are not dealing here with breaches of the law, nor with the outcomes of 'bad' legal policies; rather, we are dealing with a more extreme form of 'wrong'. It is extreme not in the sense of being based in a critique of law's content or consequences as to the production of suffering, but extreme in this sense: it is a fundamental aspect of the constitution of that which is 'normal' that law's measure makes measurement of human suffering redundant. I will look further into this shortly, but, by way of example, consider again now the situation of sanctions in Iraq which we looked at in Chapter 1. In this situation, legally authorised action resulted in the production of suffering; that suffering could not register in law as problematic precisely because it was legal. It was only damage, not injury. But that this damage could not register *as* injury—*categorically*—meant two things in light of these observations. Firstly, it meant that the *amount* of suffering was irrelevant. The increase in the number of deaths of innocents had no bearing on the matter of its being recategorised as 'injurious'. Were a thousand innocent deaths too many? No. Were 10,000 too many? No, again. Were 500,000 deaths—as turned out to be the case—too many? No. There was no measure of this sort here because *no amount of damage could cross the threshold to injury*. (Arguably, if there was any measure here, it did not relate to the extensiveness of the suffering, but to another criterion of success: whatever it takes to achieve the policy goal, the price is worth it.) These kinds of question could not be entered into, could not be calculated with, because law *precluded* that calculation; it gave, in fact, a blanket impunity where, categorically, such suffering would not register. So the question of how many would have been too many never arose. There was, in other words, an unimpeachable impunity for illimitable suffering. And the other thing to notice was this: the legality of these actions trumped any responsibility for the suffering they led to on behalf of the actors enforcing the sanctions—from the bureaucrats to the diplomats and the government ministers, they were all guiltless.

This would all sound absurd, perhaps even perverse, were it not for the facts that it is what actually happened and that this is how it was—and still is—legitimated. These are the extreme conditions of the 'normal' and they confirm a strange inversion: namely, that the harms caused by legality are far harder to combat than the harms caused by illegality.

In order to explore these insights, it is necessary to develop further the analysis as it now stands, by seeing how they can operate in practice. I will do this in the final two parts of this chapter with reference to two further case studies. These draw out, in different but related ways, the fuller implications of certain features of the juridical field to which we have just paid attention and identify further—in their practical instantiation—the specific role of foundational, as well as adjunctival, characteristics that the juridical field embodies. But before doing this, let us conclude this part of the chapter by clarifying what exactly the direct relationship between law and suffering does or does not involve.

Suffering and law's sufferance

What registers in law as a wrong? This question has a deceptively simple answer: what registers in law as a wrong is a breach of the law. Strictly speaking, then, it is not any particular loss—physical suffering, economic harm, or whatever—that registers as such, but rather only that suffering or harm that is given legal cognisance. If there is suffering that involves no breach of the law, there is no wrong. The reason that this is deceptively simple, indeed almost tautological, is because rooted in it are a number of elementary legal notions, the form and importance of which are nonetheless far from simple.

Let us begin directly with the point about the law's relation to suffering. One way of thinking about this has recently been suggested by Williams (2007) in an important article reviewing the contemporary role and prominence of human rights law. According to Williams, human rights themselves have, as their central concern, the recognition and relief of human suffering. By suffering, we normally understand, he says, both a subjective dimension of pain (physical or emotional) and an objective dimension, within which 'an observer is likely to understand and acknowledge that suffering is taking place', such as exclusion, discrimination, 'indignities', malnutrition, torture, etc. (Williams, 2007, p 138). Williams makes two observations of particular relevance to the present discussion. In line with our preceding analysis, the first is that, despite the different possible ways in which responses to human rights can be made—political, economic, or administrative, say—'it is the *legal* response' that has come, he argues:

> to dominate collective determinations of responses to suffering in the name of human rights. Law mediates these responses to a seemingly ever-expanding degree . . . the law thus provides a focal point for examining the legitimacy of human rights determinations in relation to suffering. From international norm articulation to judicial review of state practices, law and the legal process have acquired a position of pre-eminence in judging whether human rights have any purchase in a given context.
>
> (Williams, 2007, p 146)

Perhaps the main reason for this, says Williams, is that there is a commonplace assumption—borne out in practice—that, where political or moral claims appear insufficient to act as reliable motivations for acting to relieve suffering, the force of law to 'impose obligations will suffuse a particular suffering with the requirement for action' (ibid). To put this in terms we have been using here, it is the specific power of what I have called the 'juridical architecture'—the combined effect of law's claim to correctness, force and social priority—that, more than acting in accordance with any other form of obligations, makes it seem desirable to respond to suffering in such a way that will see it transformed from a damage to an injury and hence responsive to enforceable legal action.

Against this interpretation, however, Williams juxtaposes another vital one: that modern law 'is inherently *antithetical* and counter-intuitive to a notion of human rights based on the promise to relieve suffering' (ibid, emphasis added). Of course, this itself seems counter-intuitive in light of the first claim: if law can, and does, operate to recognise and act upon the demands made by human rights, how can they be *opposed* to the relief of suffering? Williams' explanation of this is that 'the law is framed by *sufferance* rather than insufferability'. Sufferance, for Williams, means 'the acknowledgment of suffering but the active toleration of its presence' or, again, 'an awareness of suffering but a determination not to act in response'. Insufferability, by contrast, would be 'an acknowledgment that a condition is intolerable, cannot be tolerated, and demands action as a consequence' (Williams, 2007, pp 146–7, emphasis added).

The essence of the claim that law is conditioned by sufferance and not insufferability lies in the point we noted at the start of this section: that what registers in law as a wrong is not suffering in itself, but the breach of a legal norm. Hence suffering has to be 'framed' within established legal categories, and has to meet the standards of recognition and response that *they* require, rather than being able to appear for what it is. It is because of the tendency of these demands—of legal categories and standards—to be highly restrictive in the recognition of suffering that Williams argues that the legal vesting of human rights shows up not as insufferability, but as sufferance. Legal structures, principles and processes combine, he argues, to form a formidable barrier to the more radical potential of human rights to demand action to relieve suffering.

Because I will come back in more detail to matters of structure and principle, although in different terms to those of Williams, let me here highlight only briefly some insightful practical examples with regard to 'process' that Williams draws from the work of Kenneth Roth, executive director of Human Rights Watch. Roth suggests that, in order for suffering to register as a legal wrong, there is a necessity to identify a 'violation, violator and remedy' (Williams, 2007, p 153). The difficulties in ascertaining, to demanding legal standards, each and every one of these factors—because if one fails, the wrong cannot be proved—mount up in an often overwhelming manner. Consider, for example, that the legal texts on which claims of infringement must necessarily be based are themselves open to interpretation and disagreement according to standard models of legal reasoning, which always acknowledge interpretative discretion, especially when the rules are themselves broadly defined. In addition to this, it is often, for reasons that we have already canvassed, difficult to identify and single out a '*violator*', and particularly so given the nature of the commission of extensive harms that rely on the organisational forms to which we have already paid attention—factors that only increase the interpretative leeway. The matter of proving that the specific violation caused the harms as alleged also faces stringent *evidentiary* tests in court proceedings, as well as a number of procedural principles routine to legal process, including safeguards for the accused, such as the right to silence. And, finally, the question of a remedy—'to ease the suffering, compensate the sufferer, or to punish the violator'—is itself usually contested or highly difficult to establish, and especially so in respect of compensation (2007, pp 153–4): to whom; for what; to be paid by whom for what? Given these features and their constant presence in legal determinations of human rights violations—and there are a number of other difficulties besides these— the upshot is that a vast amount of suffering is, in practice, treated *not* as insufferable, but rather as sufferable. It is these kinds of factors that combine to make law antithetical to the original injunction behind human rights to relieve human suffering.

These insights into the hurdles posed by procedural difficulties in the recognition of suffering are extremely important to acknowledge. As Williams rightly notes, they result in an 'ability to deflect decisions away from responsibility to take action, to challenge the human rights dimension of suffering, and to consign responsibility to an abstraction, ensur[ing] that responses are muted if not denied altogether' (2007, p 154). The complexities of legal process—sometimes technical, sometimes more mundane—work together to create an extensive and powerful set of mechanisms for disconnecting harms with responsibility for them.

That said, I think that the conclusion that Williams draws from these insights is ambivalent. He suggests that 'law is not the culprit in any perceived failure to address suffering'; rather, it 'can be interpreted as a metaphor for a general societal capacity for sufferance ... [according to which] the law merely confirms such resistance to responsibility for these conditions by maintaining its impotence, domestically and internationally, in the face of such suffering' (2007, p 156). From what I have been arguing so far, it will be clear that I am sympathetic to some aspects of these points. There is an acknowledgement that the law's cognitive techniques can, and do, block the appearance of human rights abuses and, in this sense, tend towards sufferance rather than insufferability. There is also an awareness of the fact that it is in precisely this manner that these techniques can, and do, operate as a way of dispersing and disavowing responsibilities, and that, in this sense, they correspond to a wider 'resistance to responsibility'.

But where my analysis departs from these observations is crucial: at its most basic level, the kind of harms with which I am concerned here are not those that are, as it were, committed 'elsewhere' by other forces or by people's law-breaking activities; I am not concerned with an understanding that these harms are legal violations to which the law ought to respond; I am not, or not only, concerned with the difficulties that legal techniques throw up in responding adequately (or otherwise) to these harms. Rather, it is a more radical sense that I wish to explore. It is that we should be concerned not with law's response to, but with law's involvement *in*, the *commission* of harms; we should be concerned not with problems about how law restricts acknowledgement of violations that have already taken place, but about how law actively promotes harms; I am concerned not with law's impotence, but with its *power*. In my view, it is clear that, in respect of the cases that I have considered already and will look into further now, the law is *not* a metaphor for a general tolerance of suffering, but an active component in both its commission and its cover-up. In such circumstances, it would be inadequate to say that 'law is not a culprit'. It is true, as Williams shows, that the law does indeed operate to limit or obfuscate the appearance of harms, but the kind of harms with which I am concerned here are those in which the law is *itself* implicated. Hence the inadequacy of the designation of its not being '*a culprit*' should itself be understood in a profoundly ambivalent way, a way that attests to law's *success*, not its impotence: law is both culpable in the sense of the active commission of harms and not culpable at exactly the same time. This is precisely how the disappearance of responsibility for extensive harms succeeds—and it is not through law's failure, but among the successful practices of legal responsibility. This is how the asymmetry between suffering and establishing responsibility for it operates in a legalised manner. And it is, finally, how the legally *caused* harms, not the responses to them, should best be understood: *not* as impotence, but as the system *working*.

To accept this requires a fair degree of upsetting of conventional viewpoints; it requires an acknowledgement that that which is commonly believed can, and sometimes does, promote social goods and benefits, also and at the same time is capable of producing extensive harms and covering these up. I hope that the case study I referred to in Chapter 1 gives some sense of how this may operate. But I now want to look at two further cases to show in more detail what the 'laws of irresponsibility' are and how they work. What is central to an understanding of both is that each is a perfectly normal aspect of legal ordering. Each draws on standard principles and categories of modern law, as well as on ordinary principles of legal reasoning and interpretation.

Both, however, show how these principles are capable of delivering the most brutal and extensive harms. But it is precisely in the ways in which they utilise conventional legal instruments and modes of thought and practice that they are capable of legitimating these, even to the extent of making the suffering they are complicit with appear normal or disappear. Given the identifiable and extensive nature of this suffering, it is precisely in this sense that we should understand the law, and action in accordance with it, as being 'terrifying normal'. In the next part of this chapter, I consider the colonial context and the harms that are ongoing there. In the last part, I consider the future harms of an essentially apocalyptic mode of social organisation—one that is legalised and, therefore (because law operates in an important sense to organise the future) one that is to be expected.

Part II   Colonial impunities

Historic amnesia

Nothing 'disappears' responsibility so thoroughly as the de-constitution of an empire. At least, that is, if the dissolution of the British Empire is anything to go by. One of the most successful amnesic occurrences of the twentieth century is to be found in Britain, in the erasure from public awareness by the end of the century of what had been central to it for the previous two. Churchill had led the British efforts in World War II explicitly in defence of King and Empire, and those efforts still demanded imperial massacres right through the 1950s (in Kenya, with the mass killings of the Mau Mau) and 1960s (in Aden and in the forced removals of populations in the Pacific). Indeed, right up until Churchill's death in 1965, formal Empire had continued and, even after that, the smaller scale, anti-imperial war was still going on in the north of Ireland.

This history of extermination, enslavement and cultural devastation, each part of which was carried out and sanctified according to one or more of the three guiding 'C's—commerce, Christianity and civilisation—left an indelible mark on the world. Not, of course, that very much of this would now be known by succeeding generations of schoolchildren; with an historical sense of which Stalin would have been proud, the imperial legacy was wiped out of memory so fast that, when looked at from the point of the view of Britain, its devastation might never have been real at all. Indeed, only this accounts for the even more astonishing fact that, within forty years, the British Chancellor of the Exchequer (and Prime Minister) could declare that 'the days of Britain having to apologise for its colonial history are over'—over, indeed before they had really begun—and that, instead, Britain 'should be proud' of its Empire (Milne, 2005). And only this, we might add in passing, would account for the surprise—or rather disbelief—that the invasions of Afghanistan and Iraq in the opening years of this century were abnormalities rather than part of an historical continuity.

The ways in which this erasure occurred, the factors involved and the relative success of, as well as resistance to, this erasure are manifold. They cannot be entered into here. Instead, and in line with the general argument presented here, I want to consider the role of law and legal institutions. In order to do so, I want to analyse one situation in which the English common law inheritance plays a decisive role in asserting and denying responsibilities in cases of major and extensive suffering, which continue to occur. The focus here is on the experience of Aboriginal people in Australia during and after

200 years of colonial rule. What I think is particularly important about the cases I will consider is that they are deemed to take place within an explicit transition from a colonial past to a decolonised present, one in which the highest standards of human rights, the principles of the rule of law and the institutions of democratic government are greatly valued and, so far as the rhetoric of legal justification is concerned, firmly instantiated. These cases and the issues they throw up are of central relevance and importance to the thesis developed here for a number of reasons. Firstly, they expose the manner in which legal mechanisms that promote the highest standards, etc., are involved at one and the same time in the legitimation of extensive suffering. But they do so in quite specific ways: ways that specifically deploy *basic* legal categories of common law principles and reasoning. Secondly, they give fuller and practical instantiation of the means by which processes of compartmentalisation and disassociation occur as a feature of legal thought and practice itself, and thus deepen the analysis we have been developing in earlier parts of this chapter. Moreover, they further demonstrate, in respect of a contemporary set of problems, the ways in which legal legitimation—again, through law's claim to correctness, force and social priority—operates to form a powerful bedrock on which wider social and political responses are simultaneously established and hidden from view. In this particular sense, it is important to emphasise, once again, that it is the 'normal' operation of the law with which we are concerned and that it is because of this very normality that we should not be deceived into treating this as an 'exceptional' or extreme case. As Marx (1990, p 932) pointed out, when describing systematic colonisation in the context of Australia, what is discovered here 'is not something new *about* the colonies, but, *in* the colonies'. Finally, these cases illustrate the very real impact of conceptual practices when it comes to the promotion and legitimation of suffering. That the damage, to use Hobbes's terms, cannot register as injury is precisely the conditional or constitutive sense of the irresponsibility that law can engender, which bars the question of responsibility from arising. And, in doing so, law's measure allows the suffering to continue: unremittingly, unexceptionally and without measure.

Colonial conditions

There is little doubt about the fact that past and current experiences of suffering of the Aboriginal population in Australia have their basis in the effects of dispossession and discrimination that have a continuity from the first colonial confrontations. The harms perpetuated by, and under the auspices of, the colonial regime are now well documented, as is, belatedly, the determined, if so often crushed, resistance to it. The current state of well-being of the Aboriginal population of Australia, which makes up around 2 per cent of the total population, is commonly considered to be among the worst of indigenous peoples in former British colonies, such as Canada, New Zealand and the

USA. A brief summary hardly does justice to it, but I make reference to some of the following undisputed facts.

The life expectancy of Aboriginal people is on average 17 years less than the non-Aboriginal population. According to a recent report, 'The health of Australian aboriginals is 100 years behind that of the rest of the population' (Young, 2007), with diseases that have otherwise been eradicated still being found in Aboriginal communities, including leprosy, rheumatic heart disease and tuberculosis. Infant mortality is three times that of non-Aboriginal infants. Similar disadvantages are repeated across a variety of other indicators, including access to health care, sanitation, diet and disability (HREOC, 2005). Educational opportunities are vastly poorer and adult unemployment is three times as high as among the remainder of the Australian population.

The relation between Aboriginal people and the institutions and personnel of state and federal governments has had enduring detrimental effects. A report in the 1990s by a Royal Commission on Aboriginal Deaths in Custody (RCADC, 1991) noted that Aboriginal people had 'a unique history of being ordered, controlled and monitored by the state'. That history, it continued, 'reveals a deliberate and systematic disempowerment of Aboriginal people beginning with dispossession from their land and continuing through almost every aspect of their lives' (1991, 'Overview'). The Commission had itself been set up to look into the alarming rate of deaths of Aboriginal people in detention in the years 1980–89 (a comparative figure per head of the non-Aboriginal population would have been 9,000 dying in custody in the same period). The Commission emphasised that the contemporary condition of Aboriginal people with regard to their relation to the state was one of a continuum of violence, domination and control, and thus the full and proper context for its investigation was one in which 'the over-representation of Aboriginal people in custody (and the deaths of some of them) are part of the *ongoing conflict* between "coloniser" and "colonised" ' (1991, para 10.1.3, emphasis added). The grossly disproportionate detention and incarceration rates of Aboriginal people were starkly presented in the following terms by a government report from the same period: 'The rate at which Aboriginal people are imprisoned is presently 29 times higher than that of other Australians.' While there were variations, depending on age and location, in some cases, the figures were far higher: for example, in Western Australia, the 'imprisonment rate for young Aboriginal men is more than 60 times the rate for non-Aboriginal men'. In August 1988—the year of the national celebrations of the bicentenary anniversary of British arrival on the continent—'28.6% of all detentions in police cells across Australia were Aboriginal people' (RCADC, 1991, 'Rebutting the Myths'). Despite almost 400 recommendations made by the Royal Commission, Aboriginal custody and deaths in custody as a proportion of the Australian total continued to rise throughout the 1990s.

As the Royal Commission was at pains to point out, this systematic discrimination took—and continues to take—a variety of forms: from direct formal and legal, to informal and indirectly discriminatory, practices; from earlier direct warfare, to assimilationist policies and the forcible removal of Aboriginal children from their families. Thus state and non-state racism and brutality, from 1788 to the present day, were derived from and expressed across a broad range of social practices. Aboriginal/non-Aboriginal relations, the Report therefore acknowledged, 'were entrenched not only by acts of dispossession but also by a wide variety of ideas, beliefs, and economic, legal, political and social structures which institutionalised and perpetuated them' (RCADC, 1991, para 10.1.4).

But that continuity has been met recently with a juridical response that will be our central focus here. In an effort to confront the racist assumptions on which Australian law and policy had been founded, important legal decisions from the 1990s tried to engage with, and in some respects redress, many of these assumptions as they were organised legally. One issue that arises here, then, is the extent to which systematic and profound racial discrimination may still occur in societies that are committed to legal principles of formal equality, democracy and the rule of law. It is therefore necessary to investigate whether, and how, the operation of basic principles of conventional legal reasoning may continue to be implicated in the perpetuation of harms and suffering, by operating to entrench discrimination both of the past and present. For the courts' decisions necessarily came up against—sometimes knowingly, sometimes not—questions of the limitations of how far legal mechanisms could be employed to overcome the very conditions with which they had, hitherto, been complicit. In the following section, we will look in a little detail at the Australian High Court decision in *Mabo v The State of Queensland (No 2)* (hereafter *Mabo*; paragraph pinpoints in brackets). The *Mabo* decision, given in 1992, is important for many reasons, among which are what it tells us about the very assumptions within which legal reasoning takes place and about the limits of law in addressing its colonial foundations.

Law, sovereignty and irresponsibility

Australia was colonised by the British in 1788. Sovereignty over the territory was claimed under the doctrine of *terra nullius*. According to this doctrine— which means literally 'no man's land'—land that was uninhabited could be acquired for the colonial power—in this instance, technically, the British Crown—upon being 'settled'. Of course, the Australian continent was not uninhabited; European 'settlers' had encountered the presence of an extensive Aboriginal population, as well as their resistance. In such instances, however, an 'enlarged' doctrine of *terra nullius* could still be applied by the colonising power if the following assumption was made: that 'the indigenous inhabitants were not organized in a society that was united permanently for political action' [33]. In essence, this involved an assessment by the imperial power, as the Privy Council put it in *In re Southern Rhodesia* in 1919 (cited in *Mabo* at [38]), that:

> Some tribes are so low on the scale of social organization that their usages and conceptions of rights and duties are not to be reconciled with the institutions or the legal ideas of civilized society. Such a gulf cannot be bridged.

In other words, the 'inhabitants' of *terra nullius* and their form of society were seen, from an openly racist understanding, as inferior: as Brennan CJ put it, in the leading opinion in *Mabo*, 'The indigenous people of a settled colony were thus taken to be without laws, without a sovereign and primitive in their social organization' [36].

In *Mabo*, the High Court of Australia was asked to adjudicate a claim on behalf of the Meriam people living on the Murray Islands in the Torres Straight that they had 'native title' to their land, which survived the acquisition of sovereignty by the British Crown. Assessing this claim involved the Australian High Court re-evaluating the nature and consequences of the original racist assumption on which Australia was founded and which had, for over 200 years, denied in law the existence of any such title. As Brennan CJ wrote:

> According to the cases, the common law itself took from indigenous inhabitants any right to occupy their traditional land, exposed them to deprivation of the religious, cultural and economic sustenance which the land provides, vested the land effectively in the control of the Imperial authorities without any right to compensation and made the indigenous inhabitants intruders in their own homes and mendicants for a place to live.
>
> [28]

However, Brennan CJ continued, 'Judged by any civilized standard, such a law is unjust and its claim to be part of the common law to be applied in contemporary Australia must be questioned' [28]. Accordingly, therefore, he saw that there was 'a choice of legal principle' to be made:

> This Court can either apply the existing authorities and proceed to inquire whether the Meriam people are higher "in the scale of social organization" than the Australian Aborigines whose claims were "utterly disregarded" by the existing authorities or the Court can overrule the existing authorities, discarding the distinction between inhabited colonies that were terra nullius and those which were not.
>
> [39]

According to Brennan CJ, *overruling* the precedent cases was necessary because, otherwise, their authority:

> ... would destroy the equality of all Australian citizens before the law. The common law of this country would perpetuate injustice if it were to continue to embrace the enlarged notion of terra nullius and to persist in characterizing the indigenous inhabitants of the Australian colonies as people too low in the scale of social organization to be acknowledged as possessing rights and interests in land.
>
> [63]

Brennan CJ's analysis, however, at this point encountered a duality: on the one hand, there was a recognition that 'Their [Aboriginal] dispossession underwrote the development of the [Australian] nation' [82]; on the other hand, however, he argued that, 'the *peace and order of Australian society* is built on the legal system' [29] (emphasis added) and, this being so, the court was therefore '*not* free to adopt rules that accord with contemporary notions of justice and human rights *if* their adoption would fracture the skeleton of principle which gives the body of our law its shape and internal consistency' [28]–[29] (emphasis added). In other words, the clash of principles to be adjudicated involved confronting the foundational act that dispossessed Aboriginals of their lands, while simultaneously understanding that that act was the very condition of the historical and ongoing existence of the Australian nation. How, then, could the racist founding of Australia be dealt with in accordance with contemporary principles of justice and equality, when that founding was *itself* that which gave the Australian state—and hence the law *and* the High Court—its authority?

The High Court's solution to this problem involved making a key distinction between the acquisition of sovereignty and the consequences of that acquisition. The former, it said, is not subject to review by the court; that is, the sovereignty established by the initial act of colonisation is *not justiciable* in the Australian courts. It is that very sovereignty that gives the court *its* jurisdiction to hear this case and were the matter to be justiciable—and the answer given that the act of sovereignty was invalid—then the court would undermine its own authority to make precisely such a decision. It was, however, open to the court to review the *consequences* of the acquisition of sovereignty and here was where its interpretative leeway entered. The court decided that, although sovereignty had been acquired under the doctrine of *terra nullius*, this did not mean that the Crown also acquired 'full beneficial ownership' to the whole territory. Rather, using a doctrine going back to feudal times, the Crown had acquired only a 'radical' (or ultimate, or final) title, according to which it was entitled to *grant* ownership rights even though it did not itself own the land. As Brennan CJ explained, 'What the Crown acquired was a radical title to land and a sovereign political power over land, the sum of which is not tantamount to absolute ownership of land' [55]. Radical title therefore meant that the Crown had sovereign jurisdiction to create property rights, but—and this was the key point—if no grant of ownership rights had been made to itself or another party, because the Crown did not own the land, it was possible for native title to continue to exist 'as a burden' on the radical title. It was in this space, so to speak—between radical title and full beneficial ownership—that the possibility for a native title claim could exist that survived the British acquisition of sovereignty.

In this way, where native title had not been extinguished by Crown grants of land, it was open for Aboriginal communities to show—according to the definitions that the court went on to establish—that their continued association with the land from the time of colonisation qualified them as entitled to native title rights on that land, despite the acquisition of sovereignty by the Crown over Australia. For the first time, then, and *overruling precedents* to bring Australian law in line with principles of non-discrimination, the common law was able to redress the racist implications of the doctrine of *terra nullius* and recognise native title to land.

We might consider two very different types of interpretation of this ruling. The first is congratulatory and celebrates the much-vaunted virtues of the flexibility of common law styles of reasoning. According to one commentator, the decision reflects the virtues—the 'genius' and 'spirit'—of the common law, in its ability to uphold basic standards of human rights and to respond in a pragmatic way to 'social, economic and political considerations' (Bartlett, 1993, p 181). At another level, it was also argued that the decision showed something more fundamental: namely, how the law can embody—or fail to embody—fundamental human values. On this view, what the *Mabo* decision offered for the first time in Australia was the recognition of a full humanity that had hitherto been denied to indigenous people by the law and which had, in turn, played a role in legitimating the harms of a broader social and political racism. On this reading, it was only once this full humanity was properly recognised in law that further questions of policies directed towards alleviating the suffering that Aboriginals continued to experience could be addressed. Drawing attention to this distinction, Raimond Gaita (1999) therefore concluded that:

> Fairness is at issue only when the full human status of those who are protesting their unfair treatment is not disputed ... The justice done by *Mabo* is deeper than anything that can be captured by concepts of equity as they apply to people's access to goods. It brought indigenous Australians into the constituency within which they could intelligibly press claims about unfair treatment.
>
> (Gaita, 1999, pp 81–2)

But there is a contrary view. Kerruish and Purdy (1998) make three important observations of direct relevance to our broader analysis. Firstly, they note that common law reasoning involves the application of general principles, chief among which in the *Mabo* decision were equality and formal justice (treating like cases alike). But legal equality, they argue, is intimately connected to the concept of the 'legal person'. It is this idea of modern Western law that provides a key legitimating role in so far as it operates according to the idea of treating persons as 'free and equal subjects of the law's address'. According to Kerruish and Purdy, this freedom has two aspects:

> First they are free (in the sense of stripped) of *all* their actual characteristics (from names to locations within basic social relations). Second they are supposed to have the capacity for choice or free will. Equality at law inheres in this dual freedom; that is, all those who come before the law are *equally* stripped of their actual characteristics and *equally* presumed to be responsible for their own actions.'
>
> (Kerruish and Purdy, 1998, p 150, emphasis in original)

There are two criticisms of *Mabo* that we might draw from this. First, treating people as equal before the law—referring them to, or measuring them by, the same standard—is, in fact, to treat them differently by ignoring characteristics about their identity or the context (in this instance, violent colonisation) that might be relevant under some other descriptive or normative standards. In other words, under the *dictate* of equal treatment, the force and (particularised) universality of the dominant legal system and its legal reasoning—treated as now self-evidently non-racist, equal and formally just for all Australians—can, at the same time, operate to legitimate continuing racial discrimination, inequality and ongoing dispossession through an 'active forgetting' of the historical experiences and contemporary consequences of 200 years of racial violence. Here, formal justice operates to cover this over through the 'equalising' historical trajectory that, at the same time, gives priority to the dominant perspective. Hence this operation of formal legal reasoning does not, in fact, attribute *no* identity to the legal person; rather, it imposes its version *as* an identity—in fact, as *the* only available identity—against which there is no appeal or recourse. The effect of this, as aboriginal lawyer Irene Watson has noted, is that *Mabo* 'failed to recognise difference in [the] construction of native title so as to make it fit within a western property paradigm' (Watson, 2002, p 257). The legal person is treated as given and unassailable, even if it is used to instantiate and to promote quite specific ends, such as particular understandings of (private) property. This is, no doubt, part of the function of legal personality generally, but its assumptions and implications are all the more vivid in this context, within which the harms it can cause are not so well hidden. And this point informs the second criticism: that the idea that those who come before the law are responsible for their own actions is not, in fact—and could never be, in the context of the exclusionary constructions of the colonisers' law as *Mabo* describes it—self-determined, but is rather something that is prescribed and defined *by law* itself. And yet to the extent that this *misdescribes* the historical reality, it does so in a way that nonetheless provides a legitimacy for overlooking, or in effect obliterating, this fact.

Secondly, as we have just seen, the sovereignty established by the initial act of colonisation was not justiciable in the Australian courts, because it is that sovereignty which gives the court its very jurisdiction to hear this case. Such apparently watertight logic marks the limitations of the court's power. But the effect of this is that, by refusing to engage with the acquisition of sovereignty, the original act of dispossession and its legitimacy based in racist doctrines *remains intact* as the founding act and is neither questioned, nor removed. Moreover, this foundation and its persistence—in that Aboriginal dispossession underwrote, and thus continues to underwrite, 'the development of the nation'—is now legally set in stone, but is legitimated in the present by the claim that the common law is now acting in a *non-discriminatory* manner. Thus, according to this criticism, *Mabo*, in fact, *whitewashes* responsibility for the damages caused by the invasion of Australia because, again in Watson's terms, deferral to 'doctrines of state supremacy conjure a magic, which absolves centuries of unlawfulness and violence against indigenous peoples' (Watson, 2002, p 265).

Finally, the common law conditions set out in the case (and by subsequent legislation, which has tended to restrict the conditions further) for recognition of native title, which require demonstrating continuous association with the land since the time of initial colonisation, engenders serious drawbacks and ongoing discrimination. Many Aboriginals, as a direct result of government policies, had been removed from their traditional lands either to reserves or other rural locations, or to the cities and towns. For these people, that very fact of dispossession is now legitimated by the common law's position and they thus have lost *all* possibility of their removal from their lands registering as an injury. And yet Brennan CJ's recounting of this takes a curiously passive turn: as he puts it, 'When *the tide of history has washed away* any real acknowledgment of traditional law and any real observance of traditional customs, the foundation of native title has ceased' [43] (emphasis added). As Kerruish and Perrin (1999) comment, it is precisely this metaphor that:

> conveys the legal meaning of the colonisation of Australia. Colonisation is in the past: a natural and inevitable force. The law of native title, on the other hand, is in a present that, while absolved from any responsibility for that which has been washed away, acknowledges the possibility of survival.
>
> (Kerruish and Perrin, 1999, p 3)

Hence these—perhaps the majority of—dispossessed Aboriginals are instead now treated by the law equally as Australian citizens, their dispossession failing to register in law at all. As such, as Kerruish and Purdy conclude:

> the Australian common law has now managed to strip those Aboriginal people whose connection with the land has been broken of the identity at law of native inhabitants of Australia. It is a *further act of colonisation* that compounds dispossession by non-recognition of Aboriginal identity.
>
> (Kerruish and Purdy, 1998, p 162, emphasis added)

Consequently, the only kind of Aboriginal identity that *would* be recognised was one that was able to prove continuous connection with a particular area of land, that land being the same land that had been occupied by them prior to 1788 and unbrokenly since then, and on which traditional practices and customs had also been continuously and demonstrably observed. The restrictiveness of this test related not only to difficulties of proof, but involved a remarkably limiting definition of what would count as 'Aboriginality' for the purposes of native title. As Stewart Motha (2007) puts it, the only available identity of the successful native title applicant would be that declared by the law to be a 'proper' or 'authentic native', one whose current and historical provenance had to be proved to the satisfaction of a tribunal, whereby it guaranteed that the 'recognition by the common law depends on the natives being sufficiently native' (2007, pp 74–5). With this remarkably patronising, if nonetheless powerful, definition, Motha concludes, 'the overarching political power of "one sovereignty", "one law" and the homogenising drive of a "civilised society" is reiterated in the name of justice and human rights' (2007, p 74).

In the result, not only would connection with the land be, in most cases, impossible to show (as the court well knew, this was the consequence of these very colonial practices), but, even in those few cases in which connection might still be shown, further hurdles lay ahead. In particular, the standards of proof required by the common law to establish the existence of native title relied heavily on documentary evidence, which would inevitably be prejudicial to its discovery. The specific drawback here related not only to the fact that Aboriginal culture was an oral one, but that the only documentary evidence likely to be available was that compiled by white settlers themselves. The effective result of this evidentiary hurdle—as was, in fact, borne out in subsequent native title cases, such as *Yorta Yorta*—was that 'There would be no other evidence than that *of* colonialism' (Kerruish and Perrin, 1999, p 5, emphasis in original).

From these observations, we may witness the power of common law reasoning, its legal concepts and interpretative techniques, in legitimating—on the *very grounds* of equality, freedom and formal justice—ongoing dispossession and an effective disavowal of the past. This is the power of legal reasoning in a colonial context, even where democratic and non-discriminatory principles are espoused. While the damages and inequalities that exist in Australia for Aboriginal people are ongoing, the integrity of the common law remains intact through the legal declaration of what effectively amounts to 'colonialism without (bad) consequences'. Without bad consequences, that is, for the colonisers. This is what happens, as Aboriginal writer Kevin Gilbert (1978) put it, 'When the thief is the judge'.

Yet there is one final twist to this case to which we need to pay attention and it is central to the thesis developed here. It concerns the way in which the High Court sought to disavow *its*—that is, the common law's—responsibility for any past and present harms by transferring them onto the political state in a very specific way. Brennan CJ had stated earlier in his judgment that:

> it would be a curious doctrine to propound today that, when the benefit of the common law was first extended to Her Majesty's indigenous subjects in the Antipodes, its first fruits were to strip them of the right to occupy their ancestral lands.
>
> [39]

(Let us leave to stand for themselves the calamitous ironies of those terms '*benefit*', '*curious*' and '*fruit*', except for succumbing to the temptation to say that it was, indeed, a strange fruit.) The purpose of this way of presenting the matter was that it allowed Brennan CJ to build towards the conclusion that it was *not* an effect of the common law that dispossessed indigenous Australians, but rather 'the exercise of a sovereign authority over land exercised recurrently by Governments' [68]. Even if, he goes so far to stress the point, no native title were ever to be found, it is still:

> appropriate to identify the events which resulted in the dispossession of the indigenous inhabitants of Australia, *in order to dispel the misconception* that it is the common law rather than the actions of governments which made many of the indigenous people of this country trespassers on their own land.
>
> [39] (emphasis added)

Why was there such a tenacious determination to dispel this misconception and what effect would it have? The answer is two-fold. On the one hand, the common law of Australia would be granted, albeit by itself, an absolution from any responsibility for the harms done to Aboriginal people—it was, no less, to be the very agent of rectification, the redeemer of the values of equality and decency that governments had done so much to denigrate. On the other hand, however, there was this sting in the tail: because the act of government that asserted sovereignty in the first place was not justiciable, transferring responsibility for dispossession to it meant that dispossession and all of the harms that followed from it immediately vanished beyond the horizon of legal responsibility. In formulating it in this way, Brennan CJ could establish that dispossession was 'not a matter for which law is responsible or accountable' (Motha, 2007, p 76). The common law thus transferred responsibility for the deeds and consequences of colonialism away from itself to acts of government, and deems them legally untouchable according to the law of the land. And what of the political or state responsibility for its colonial acts of dispossession? This, too, was untouchable for one unassailable reason: as the High Court acknowledged, the state and its institutions, indeed the very 'Australian nation' depended—*and depends*—constitutively on the dispossession of Aboriginal peoples. It cannot engage that dispossession—it cannot put itself in a position of responsibility—without dispossessing itself. Here, in other words, and we see now how it draws on several aspects of what we have paid attention to previously, was a case of the disappearance of responsibility *par excellence*. And it forces us to pay heed to the important insight of Anghie (1999) when he notes that 'no adequate account of sovereignty can be given without analyzing the constitutive effect of colonialism on sovereignty'. That is, we should note, *not* the effect of sovereignty on colonialism, but rather something far more profound and enduring: that 'Colonialism cannot be accounted for as an example of the application of sovereignty; rather, sovereignty was constituted and shaped through colonialism' (Anghie, 1999, p 6). This is the organisation of irresponsibility—the inability to have the question of responsibility raised at all—at its most powerful.

Good intentions

The *Mabo* decision did not have a great deal to say about intention. Indeed, what it did directly say about it immediately drew it up into the realms of the apparently absurd. I will not dwell on this here; suffice to point out what the difficulty was. The court had reasoned that, in order for native title to be extinguished, there should be a clear and express intention to do so. The difficulty was, however, that there could be no proof of such intention. This was not because of evidentiary problems; rather, it was because, up until 1992—that is, until the court gave its judgment—native title—so far as successive governments and courts, and indeed everybody, had been concerned—was entirely non-existent. There could, therefore, be no intention to extinguish something that did not exist. This put the court in something of an awkward position. Given that native title had to have had existed from the time of initial colonial contact, even though no one had, until now, recognised it, the intention had therefore and likewise to be attributed retrospectively. Intention to extinguish native title, although factually non-existent, could thus be imputed to acts of governments that operated inconsistently with the existence of native title (as they inevitably would have done if only native title had been recognised).

There is, indeed, something of the 'magical' in all of this and that sense of magic is not purely metaphorical. In operation here is a fiction—a legal fiction—according to which something that is known, in fact, not to be the case is assumed in law to be the case. Despite its avowedly fictional quality, this can have very real and very important legal consequences, and hence very real and important practical consequences that are legitimated on the basis of the fiction. The device of legal fictions is something widely accepted, if not frequently used, by lawyers and courts. In this particular instance, however, its existence is deployed to legitimate a changed understanding of the past; indeed, it is used to legitimate a *rewriting* of that past as one that is now fictionally aware of the presence of native title. That the court is still keen to talk about intention in such circumstances is a mark both of the importance of intention in the mindset of legal practice, but also of the way in which what intention is, or amounts to—quite clearly—a matter of legal attribution rather than of discovery. This latter point is inevitably true when it comes to the intention of institutions, such as governments, which, at least beyond the realms of legal fiction, could never have intentions in the way they would ordinarily be understood. But, for our purposes, the significant point is not simply the recognition of this, but rather that of how intention can be used as another 'normative device', which can be used in ways that respond to and legitimate particular interests or needs. In so being used, it becomes a means of asserting or denying something, according to which actions and their consequences take on a particular hue when they are matched up with a specific intention. That is, the meaning of an action can be read off the intention *even though* that intention is a legal fabrication. The symbolic effectiveness that comes with the notion of intention—as a part of the long trajectory of responsibility in modernity that we considered in Chapter 2—thus plays a key role, a part of which, in this case, is to distinguish the acts of government from the desired absolution of the common law in the practices of dispossession.

But intention is, of course, a double-edged sword: the role that intention plays is of widespread consequence not only in the colonial context, but generally. Intention, and particularly 'good intentions'—or, at least, not 'bad intentions'—have a potent legitimation function in the disavowal of actions that knowingly or foreseeably result in harms. The search for intentions, whether real or fictionalised, accounts for an important way in which immunity from attributions of responsibility occurs; when intention is built into a legal definition, not finding it is one important way of making responsibility disappear. This, as I have suggested, is a widespread phenomenon, the presence of which is rooted in modern legal thought; it recalls Calasso's (1994) observation about the distinction between '*the evil of the mind and the evil of the deed, murder and death*'. Its centrality to law is, as Hannah Arendt (1977, p 277) put it when writing in the context of the Eichmann trial, that there is an 'assumption current in all modern legal systems that intent to do wrong is necessary for the commission of a crime. On nothing, perhaps, has civilized jurisprudence prided itself more than on this taking into account of the subjective factor'. But while this is taken commonly as an elementary principle of criminal law, when we consider its more general impact—particularly in the case of large-scale commissions of harms—its effect is not to make secure responsibilities, but rather the opposite: to engender impunities.

Sometimes, this is explicit. To recall an example mentioned earlier, when the consequences of the extensive deployment of military force include the gross violation of human rights of civilian populations, those very violations are trumped—legalised, so to speak—according to the doctrine that legitimates civilian deaths ('collateral damage' as it is commonly now referred to), under which the military action in question was proportionate and did not intentionally target civilians. Here, a lack of intention covers a multitude of killings. Of course, this leads to all kinds of deeply problematic issues if logical or principled consistency is valued, which, in this instance, it cannot be (at least, if the practices of states are to be recognised for what they are and do). There is, perhaps, no better statement of the kind of topsy-turvy moral problems that legalised killing induces—at least, for those who are committing them—than in the reported consternation of an American Vietnam war soldier:

> it was morally right to shoot an unarmed Vietnamese who was running, but wrong to shoot one who was standing or walking; it was wrong to shoot an enemy prisoner at close range, but right for a sniper at long range to kill an enemy soldier who was no more able to defend himself; it was wrong for infantrymen to destroy a village with white-phosphorous grenades, but right for a fighter pilot to drop napalm on it.
>
> (Bourke, 2000, p 203)

What is key in matters of intention is that, while the intention may or may not exist as a matter of psychological fact, the question of its attribution is crucial. But that attribution takes it cue, as it were, from the interests that guide the desired outcome—the finding or negation of unlawfulness—rather than from any notion of intentional responsibility *per se*. To think of it the other way round is, so to speak, to put the cart before the horse: it is to see responsibility as separable from its function as a 'normative device'.

With this preliminary observation in mind and to make clear the very real importance of this issue, let us return to the Australian context and contrast the fictional intention found in the *Mabo* decision with another Australian High Court case, according to which intention could *not* be read off from the consequences of the practices of government, no matter how devastating these consequences were. The case with which we are concerned here is what is known more widely as that of the 'Stolen Generations'. And the contrast is striking.

The forcible removal of Aboriginal children from their families was an important element of the policies of absorption and assimilation that Australian governments promoted throughout most of the twentieth century, right up until the 1960s. These removals were widespread and enduring. They were authorised by legal instruments. In a harrowing report written by the Human Rights and Equal Opportunities Commission (HREOC, 1997), many Aboriginal survivors testified, often with great personal difficulty, to the nature of their experiences and the harms they suffered as a result of their removal as children under government policies. The removal of children from families has, as might be expected, a profound impact on their emotional, psychological and familial well-being. It profoundly affects interpersonal, as well as longer term intergenerational, relations. In the context of the Australian programmes, the children, once removed, were also commonly subjected to different forms of abuse ranging from extreme physical and sexual abuse, to endemic racism and forced employment. They were also the object of intense personal controls and limitations with respect to movement, marriage and education.

Part of the inspiration behind these policies lay in openly eugenic ideas about the inferiority of the Aboriginal race and in the belief that it was a 'dying race' whose end was inevitable. While believing that the 'full-blood' Aboriginal culture would quickly die out as a result of its technological and civilisational inferiority, Aboriginal extinction, it was argued, would be hastened by policies that operated to separate from their families 'half-caste' children, as one means of 'whitening out' Aboriginal culture as a distinctive identity by not allowing it to be reproduced over time. As Dr Cecil Cook, an 'Aboriginal Protector' in the Northern Territory in the late 1920s explained:

> Generally by the fifth and invariably sixth generation, all native characteristics of the Australian Aborigines are eradicated. The problem of our half-castes will be quickly eliminated by the complete disappearance of the black race, and the swift submersion of their progeny in the white . . . The Australian native is the most easily assimilated race on earth, physically and mentally.
>
> (HREOC, 1997, p 137)

In light of the laws and policies that guided these practices, and the evidence that the Commission received from those who came before it to testify, the 'Stolen Generations' Report concluded in the following stark terms (1997, p 266): 'the Australian practice of Indigenous child removal involved both systematic racial discrimination and genocide as defined by international law.' The former legal designation—systematic racial discrimination—was hardly likely to be contestable, because these practices fitted within general and explicit government policies of discrimination, something perhaps most prominently known in respect of the fact that Aboriginal people were excluded from basic citizenship rights until the 1960s. In terms of the latter legal category—genocide—the Report argued that the Australian governmental practices met the terms of the 1948 Genocide Convention, under which genocide is defined as 'acts committed with intent to destroy, in whole or in part, a national, ethnical, racial, or religious group' by (among other means), 'forcibly transferring children of the group to another group' (Art 2(e)). Although it is associated in the public eye with mass killings directed at particular ethnic or racial groups, this does not exhaust the legal definition of genocide. As this situation showed, the destruction of a group can come about not through killing, but through making the reproduction of that group impossible. And it is in this sense, the Report concluded, that the legal policies of the 'Stolen Generations' amounted to genocide.

In the same year as this report was published, a case reached the High Court of Australia in which a number of Aboriginal claimants sought to gain legal recognition that the legislation that had authorised the removal of five of them as children breached their constitutional rights: *Kruger v Commonwealth* (1997). The claimants also raised, and the court adjudicated, the question of whether the legal practices authorising the forcible removals that had taken place in such circumstances amounted to genocide. The case is a complex one, based mainly around matters of Australian constitutional law and statutory interpretation. I will not attempt to do justice to that complexity here, but will focus only on the aspect of intention, as discussed by the judges.

One of the key early pieces of legislation that applied in the Northern Territory was the Aboriginals Ordinance of 1918, under which five of the claimants had been removed from their families (the sixth claimant was the mother of a child who had been removed). They challenged its constitutionality on the grounds that it infringed certain rights enshrined in the Constitution, common law or in international law. This Ordinance had authorised not only the power to take children away from their families, but a whole panoply of regulations, many of the most stringent of which concerned girls and women: 'Aboriginal females were under the total control of the Chief Protector from the moment they were born until they died unless married and living with a husband "who is substantially of European origin".' (Such marriages required the permission of the Chief Protector.) In addition, they could be 'removed from their families at any age and placed in an institution. They could be sent out to work at a young age and never receive wages. They had no right of guardianship over their own children who could be similarly taken from them' (HREOC, 1997, pp 133–4). But it was specifically with respect to s 6(1) of the Ordinance that the court laid emphasis. This section had conferred a legal power on the 'Chief Protector of Aboriginals' to remove Aboriginal children from their families 'if, in his opinion it is necessary or desirable in the interests of the aboriginal or half-caste for him to do so'.

It was in light of this aspect of the law that the Court decided that *no* intention to commit genocide (as it was defined in the relevant article of the

Genocide Convention noted above) could be found. The rejection of the claimants' position in this respect was stated plainly by Dawson J. He judged that it was:

> not possible to conceive of any acceptable definition of genocide which would embrace the actions authorised by the 1918 Ordinance, given that they were required to be performed in the best interest of the Aboriginals concerned or of the Aboriginal population.
>
> *Kruger v Commonwealth* [161]

Despite the ravages visited upon the Aboriginal communities and, in particular, its children, all of which was well documented, no intention to commit harm could be read back from these harmful consequences to inform the understanding of the law. Here, the wording of s 6(1) of the 1918 Ordinance trumped any alternative understanding of the reality. Or, to put it differently, the 'good intentions' of those who enforced a law, believing it to be 'in the best interests' of children—identifiable as part of a group solely according to racial characteristics—to be removed en masse from their families, homes and culture for the purpose of hastening the end of their race, and who were subject to further intense discrimination and abuse as a consequence, did not register as at all problematic according to Australian law and its principles. The fact is, however, that *no amount* of such suffering would have allowed the translation of harm into legally recognisable injury. The measure of *that* translation—one forever denied by this case and for these, and all other similar, claimants—lay exclusively in the interpretation of a legal expression of good intentions.

A few years after this case, two Aboriginal claimants sought to pursue a claim for damages for their forcible removal as children, this time not in public law, but in a private law action. The Australian government threw millions of dollars at legal teams to defend itself against the claim. It argued, among many other things, that, because of the claimants' delay in bringing the action, the government was being prejudiced against in allowing the case even to be heard. But the case was heard. The claimants lost it, as they did their appeal: *Cubillo v Commonwealth* [2000]. I happened to sit in the court one day in Darwin. Watching the proceedings, although not listening to the claimants, the philosophical claim of Lyotard (1988, p 9) became visible before my eyes: '*the conflict that opposes* [the parties] *is done in the idiom of one of the parties while the wrong suffered by the other is not signified in that idiom.*' It was not so much that the claimants and other witnesses could not be heard; rather, it was that, no matter what they said, they would not be able prove their claim. The law, as in the case literally of *Mabo*, captured the field, in this instance, of all possible discourses of responsibility and this was its profound irresponsibility.

At the time of these reports and cases, the Australian Prime Minister, John

Howard, was invited to make an apology for the suffering of the 'Stolen Generations'. He refused. He said one can only meaningfully apologise for something one *did*. This refusal was widely condemned, including by the other political parties. But it embodies a number of crucial truths. Most plainly, it denoted a *continuity* with, not a breach of, standards of justice to be found and honoured in the Australian common law (and the Western common law tradition, of which it is a part). It does so, moreover, on the basis of a view of responsibility that, as we saw in Chapter 2, is an affirmation of an agency-based or individualist logic within which one is only responsible for that which one intends or has negligently caused. In this instance, this under-standing is used—as a normative device—to compartmentalise responsi-bilities, but it does so in profoundly asymmetrical ways. According to the image of the two-way mirror, all kinds of current benefits that are built on the 'achievements' of the past—from landholding, all the way to taking patriotic pride in the nation's past—can be held onto or espoused as 'one's own', even though 'our current' generation did not *do* any of those things either. There is, in other words, a simultaneous acceptance of benefits accruing from, and a refusal to accept responsibility for any wrongdoing having occurred in, the self-same period.

Finally, this case shows up—as clearly as any case we will look at—that what underpins this, what gives this irresponsibility its greatest legitimacy, are the legal doctrines on which the whole edifice rests. It confirms what I have pointed out in several places already, hopefully now with considerably more clarity and force: namely, that the notion of any moral or political norms as somehow separate or separable from the basic categories and forms of action, the elementary forms of economic and legal organisation that a society has rooted at its core, is deeply implausible. The dominant morality finds its opportunities and limitations only superficially on the fundamental struc-tures of social and legal organisation, and the policies they foster—and as long as these conditions endure, there is no morality free from their taint.

We might finally reflect on both the power and the limits of modern legal thought by asking whether, and to what extent, principles of modern law and legal reasoning are able to redress the effects of colonial and deeply dis-criminatory practices when these very principles have been, and continue to be, themselves complicit in the legitimation of these discriminatory practices. As a short coda to this section, then, we should acknowledge in passing one objection that can be raised in such contexts: namely, would a repeal of the law—a change to the content of the law along the lines begun, say, by *Mabo*—not provide a way of redressing that which has hitherto been denied, or unable to register, as suffering? This may, at first glance, appear a plausible objection. But to understand how fundamentally inadequate it is, we need only consider, by way of summarising this part, what we have seen lies at the root of the problems here. These include, among other features: the forms of sovereignty and property distinctive to Western legal conceptions, of which the Australian version is merely an instantiation; the elementary categories of legal personality and principles of legal reasoning that are deployed to justify the legal conclusions we have noted; the relation between law and politics that each of these, in their own ways, involves. Could any change in the law, any repeal of the law, really be understood as getting at these fundamental conceptions, and the forms of social and institutional ordering they promote? This seems highly implausible. As the High Court stated clearly in *Mabo*, any change in the laws cannot be allowed to shake the very foundations on which such change rests. As Brennan CJ put it: the 'skeleton of principle which gives the body of our law shape and internal consistency' can be 'modified' but it cannot be 'destroyed' [29]. The fundamental tenets of the law—of the elementary categories and conceptions just listed that constitute, so to speak, the law's very DNA—cannot be removed. Repeal will not, and cannot be allowed to, amount to destruction. It is in exactly this sense, as Brennan CJ stated in an undoubtedly profound yet merciless reflection, that 'Our law is the prisoner of history' [29]. And so too are those who live under it.

Part III   Apocalyptic jurisprudence

Global irresponsibility

We have considered so far the ways in which legal norms organise irresponsibility explicitly in terms of harms in the present and the past. Because law is centrally concerned with the ordering of behaviour in the future, we would expect to find its irresponsible capabilities, so to speak, extending there too. It is to this that we now turn. The focus in this part will be on the interpretation of the legality of nuclear weapons as, perhaps, the ultimate instantiation of law's ability to legitimate possible future harms on a massive scale. But before turning to this, we might see both the nature and extent of such harms as part of a global environmental concern in which modern legal institutions also play a central role.

Ulrich Beck, whose work we touched on in Chapter 2, has written extensively about the way in which modern institutions in what he has termed contemporary '*risk society*' organise and manage, or fail to manage, risks on a global level. Risk society, writes Beck, is a catastrophic society: one in which the technological developments of modernity produce risks of such magnitude and potentially enduring environmental devastation that they threaten all living beings on the planet. While scientific progress may have led, in the West at any rate, away from a society of scarcity, it is now precisely in terms of wealth and *over*production that contemporary risks appear most prevalent. Whether in terms of environmental pollution and global warming, nuclear radiation, or genetic modification and toxins in food, the risks associated with each of these arise as, or produce, hazards that put in jeopardy the very successes of the modernity from which they flow. As Beck puts it, 'at the turn of the twenty-first century the unleashed process of modernization is over-running and overcoming its own coordinate system', and it this, he argues, which signals that we have now entered a period of 'reflexive modernity', one in which modernity itself 'is becoming its own theme' (Beck, 1992, pp 19, 87).

That these developments represent a major, and possibly irreversible, shift from earlier phases of modernity, says Beck, involves recognising a number of factors, including that: what is so specifically dangerous and novel about the nature of the hazards associated with reflexive modernity is that they are incalculable; such risks are often difficult to detect, both spatially and tem-porally, until they cause harms and hence affect the future in ways that are highly unpredictable; accordingly, they tend to be difficult to delimit 'and thus affect not only producers and consumers but also (in the limiting case) all other "third parties", including those as yet unborn' (Beck, 1995, p 77). Given this, as well as the fact that it may be impossible to single out particular 'perpetrators', traditional calculations about cause, effect and attribution of fault all turn out to be highly problematic. Moreover, risks such as those associated with environmental degradation or global warming tend not to respect national boundaries and so the traditional boundaries or 'borders' of jurisdiction become increasingly irrelevant; while they are not dissociable from existing structures of wealth and power, such hazards no longer conform to these in traditional ways. As Beck succinctly puts it, 'poverty is hierarchic, smog is democratic' (Beck, 1992, p 36).

Given these observations, it seems plausible to think that traditional legal concepts and categories may themselves become impotent in the face of global ecological threats. Thus, conventional legal categories of causation, individual liability and foreseeability of harm are no longer adequate con-ceptual means of redressing the harms of risk society. In the face of incalcul-able threats and in situations in which the identities of victims and perpetrators merge, modernity's legal mechanisms for dealing with risk allocation might be thought to provide inadequate resources. Moreover, the relation between law, politics and science itself may be thought to be reconfigured in ways that challenge the very ability of legal and political accountability to organise with regard to the dangers faced and ways of dealing with them. Because risks tend to be 'knowledge based', that is they are 'open to social definition and construction', they can, says Beck, 'be changed, magnified, dramatized or minimized within knowledge' (1992, p 23). What this means is that they are open to conflictual understandings in such a way that the *politics* of the definition of risks become a crucial feature of attempts to acknowledge or alleviate them.

One of the central problems here is the emergence of an asymmetry between the production of, and knowledge about, risks and responsibility for them, which plays out directly in the context of the relationship between law and politics, and science and business. As Beck maintains:

> The structuring of the future is taking place indirectly and unrecogniz-
> ably in research laboratories and executive suites, not in the parliament or
> in political parties . . . politics is becoming a publicly financed advertising
> agency for the sunny sides of a development it does not know, and one
> that is removed from its active influence.
>
> (Beck, 1992, pp 223–4)

Yet this asymmetry is compounded by the fact that, at the level of social
expectations, governments and states are still seen as the key players in legitimating the practices and consequences of scientific 'progress', even when, in
fact, they are ill equipped to do so. Where government is still perceived as the
main port of call in terms of trying to alleviate or compensate for harms
caused, the consequence is that 'As side effects the risks fall under the
responsibility of politics and not business. That is to say, business is not
responsible for something it causes, and politics is responsible for something
over which it has no control' (Beck, 1992, p 227). In this respect, and with
potentially devastating consequences, we encounter a further instantiation of
the phenomenon of 'responsibility transference' discussed earlier.

But there is one more key observation that might be made about the role of
law in risk society and it is a far more devastating account of its role than one
of mere inadequacy or impotence. Instead, it suggests that law and legal
institutions may themselves be complicit in the ongoing production and normalisation of global risks. If so, then we are confronted by the possibility not
only of law's inability to confront global hazards, but by the fact that they
operate, in fact, to promote them. If modern industrial society is centrally
concerned with the distribution of goods, notes Beck, then risk society is
concerned with the distribution of 'bads'. But such distribution takes place
according to certain dynamics, including (importantly) that of legal regulation. Yet in this instance, instead of law operating, as would more commonly
be understood, to promote responsible behaviour, to set standards and
impose sanctions consequent on their breach, the actual operation of law
turns out to be a way of organising *irresponsible* behaviour. In other words,
dangerous actors—whether states or corporations—carry out activities that
contribute to the global production of hazards, but such harmful activities
are *legalised* through a regime that claims still to be there to protect people
and the environment from such harms. The reason that this happens in this
scenario is because the legal principles for organising responsibility—in particular, those regarding causation, individual liability and proof—are rooted
in an earlier form of modernity and have not caught up with the nature and
extent of the dangers now being faced. Thus, their operation is not only
inadequate, but contributes to the problem. This, says Beck, is the 'concealed
gap of the century' and, in the context of ecological harms, it leads, in actual
fact, to nothing less than 'legalized universal pollution' (Beck, 1995, p 131).

By assigning responsibilities only under certain well-established legal categories, then, what modern law and legal institutions do is organise a system of *non*-liability, a regime of unaccountability: environmental harms continue at an alarming rate and yet either no one at all can be, or is, held responsible for them or (what amounts in effect to much the same thing) responsibility is massively asymmetrical to the harms caused (small fines, say, for massive damage caused, etc.). The overall effect of this globally is summed up by Beck in the following terms:

> If one wanted to think up a system for turning guilt into innocence, one could take this collaboration between justice, universal culpability, acquittal and pollution as one's model. Nothing criminal is happening here, nothing demonstrably criminal anyway. Its undemonstrability is guaranteed precisely by compliance with, and strict application of, the fundamental rule of justice—the principle of individual culpability, whereby both pollution and non-pollution, justice and (coughing) injustice, are guaranteed.
>
> (Beck, 1995, p 135)

In this way, modern law is not simply inadequate to the task of combating the dangers of risk society; rather, it is also directly involved in *perpetuating* their ongoing development. This, says Beck, shows how law in risk society engineers a global system of *organized irresponsibility*.

I want now to follow through some of these general observations in the specific context of the human and environmental threats posed by nuclear weapons. Clearly, they share some important characteristics with the kind of threats just identified, although in some respects the role of modern law and legal institutions is more direct and powerful with regard to these nuclear threats. But this is partly why I would like to focus on this case: because no matter how direct, visible and undisputed a presence these threats contain, it does not affect the way in which law's role continues to organise irresponsibility, with all the potentially disastrous results that this entails.

The nuclear presence

The issue of the legality of nuclear weapons will be discussed in this context and I set out the ways in which they develop the argument of this book in what follows. But nuclear weapons, if and when we do think about them, have a visceral quality that sometimes seems to exceed rational argument. Indeed, this is part of the issue in the following analysis. Moreover, there tends to be an 'elephant in the room' quality about nuclear weapons that pervades social and political life generally, and academic writing in particular. For example, Stanley Cohen's (2001) recent well-received book on 'states of denial' makes no mention of them and, likewise, although there has been a strand in recent philosophical literature concerned with the 'disaster', in terms of twentieth-century genocides and other mass atrocities, strangely nuclear weapons feature rarely, if at all, in such discourse. These silences and omissions are, to some extent, merely representative of a broader problem. So there are two preliminary observations to which I would like to draw attention.

The first is an objection: that the 'matter' of nuclear weapons has now become a slightly dated focus. The arms race of the Cold War, along with its attendant policies—first strike, deterrence, mutual assured destruction, etc.—have themselves gone cold. The times at which civil preparation for nuclear strikes from the Soviet Union included striking fear into the hearts and minds of generations of schoolchildren belong to a different era. The new geo-political world disorder no longer makes sense in these terms (of course, for most people it never *did* make sense in these terms). Moreover, the nature of warfare has changed, the future of conflict is mutating away from the full-scale threats of the high era of nuclear posturing and, thus, the issue of nuclear annihilation is far less of a concern today.

While some of this may be true, it is nevertheless the case that, for all kinds of reasons, 'weapons of mass destruction' have indeed now re-emerged on the radar of public and governmental consciousness. (Of course, the issue, like the bombs, had never gone away.) One reason for this is because it is generally accepted that nuclear proliferation is likely to increase. The practice of nuclear states themselves—the USA, UK, France, Russia, China, India, Pakistan and Israel—does nothing to signal otherwise. For example, US funding for developing tactical 'bunker-busting' nuclear warheads continues and the attitude that asserts its 'nuclear primacy' has seen belief that a nuclear conflict can be won again gaining ground (see Lieber and Press, 2006). There are adaptations, not reversals, of nuclear policy from the Cold War position that have seen moves towards the development of 'a family of smaller and more flexible strike plans designed to defeat today's adversaries', as well as the upgrading of existing nuclear forces, including treating aging weapons to 'life-extension' programmes (NRDC, 2006, p 71). (The horrors that nuclear weapons discourse effects on ordinary language and common sense can never be out-ironied, with its *'families'* and *'life extensions'*; the USA's 'Nuclear Posture' Review claimed that 'Nuclear nations have a responsibility to assure the safety and reliability of their own nuclear weapons' (USNPR, 2001, p 55) and Jack Straw, British Cabinet Minister, urged us to realise that 'mutually assured destruction can help in certain circumstances to calm the world' (Woodward, 2006).)

In 2007, the UK government committed itself to replacing its Trident nuclear programme, the cost of which to the British taxpayer will be at least £75bn. In addition to this, of course, a form of nuclear weaponry has already been normalised in recent conflicts: namely, the use of depleted uranium shells by US and UK armed forces, the impact of which, in terms of radiation fallout, is well documented, particularly with regard to both recent Gulf

Wars. In fact, the foreign policy approaches of nuclear countries to the perceived threats of nuclear proliferation—especially, currently, in respect of
Iran and North Korea, but also with regard to non-state groups, such as
Al-Qaeda—suggest that *they* believe that proliferation is likely. The failure to
secure agreement on moves towards disarmament at the Nuclear Non-
Proliferation Treaty review process in New York in 2005 merely confirmed
these deep-seated problems.

At root, perhaps, it is the (universalised) logic of deterrence to which the
nuclear powers have held that makes comprehensible the belief that the best
way to prevent attack by another power is, in fact, to *have* nuclear weapons—
and it is all the more so, and all the more justifiable, as we shall see, if this
possession is legal. On this defensive account alone, and not thinking further
about motives of aggression, nuclear proliferation is likely.

The second observation is one that I expect will have some resonance for
the reader. Here is how Jonathan Schell (1982) expressed it, writing of his
experience in the 1970s and 1980s:

> Thoughts of the nuclear peril were largely banned from waking life, and
> relegated to dreams or to certain fringes of society, and open, active
> concern about it was restricted to certain "far out" people, whose ideas
> were on the whole not so much rejected by the supposedly sober, "real-
> istic" people in the mainstream as simply ignored. In this atmosphere,
> discussion of the nuclear peril even took on a faintly embarrassing aura,
> as though dwelling on it were somehow melodramatic, or were a sopho-
> moric excess that serious people outgrew with maturity.
>
> (Schell, 1982, pp 150–1)

This latter observation undoubtedly still resonates. Certainly augmented by
the first observation concerning the end of the Cold War, there prevails a
feeling still that discussion of nuclear weapons and their destructive power is
indeed melodramatic, still too 'far out', still an immature, even an irrational,
excess that should not disturb politics as usual. And yet, concludes Schell in
his insightful and disturbing book, that 'we try to make do with a Newtonian
politics in an Einsteinian world . . . is the source of our immediate peril'
(1982, p 188).

For Schell, then, this calmness betrays not a maturity, but rather a collective insanity: 'an insanity that consist[s] not in screaming and making a com-
motion but precisely in *not* doing these things in the face of overwhelming
danger, as though everyone had been sedated' (1982, p 151, emphasis in
original). It says a great deal about the mentality and social structures of
denial that this sense of immature excess *continues* to be a common one, both
in academic and general public discourse. I expect, in fact, that many readers
will already have a feeling that the problem is exaggerated. But, as I hope will
become clear, this denial—in which, again, legal structures play a significant

role—represents an extraordinary achievement in the social amnesias that cloud contemporary social thought and practice.

So let me begin this section by drawing attention to some key features of the nuclear age in terms of their potential harms. Perhaps the most crucial thing here is to understand the radical *discontinuity* between the non-nuclear and nuclear ages. The 'nuclear world' ushered in a qualitatively different era of human history; the human ability to harness the power trapped in atoms changed the very nature of our presence on the planet. Technological development has always been absolutely central to understanding changes in human interaction and the institutional forms it takes—there is nothing new in this. As Zizek (2001a, p 137) reminds us, for example: 'Marx's recurrent theme is that the steam engine and other eighteenth century technological innovations did much more to revolutionise the whole of social life than all that century's spectacular political events.' But the development of nuclear technology and weaponry is *categorically* different from any previous development. We may recall Oppenheimer's immediate insight on witnessing the first atomic test—'*I am become death, the destroyer of worlds*'—or the Einstein-Russell Manifesto of 1955, which addressed itself not to any political creed or institution, but to all people as 'members of a biological species': if nuclear weapons were used, it emphasised, 'there will be universal death, sudden only for a minority, but for the majority a slow torture of disease and disintegration'.

It is this '*universal death*' that signifies the discontinuity. Figures often seem cold, but consider briefly the following: one 20 megaton bomb represents more destructive capacity—more than 1,600 times that unleashed over Hiroshima —than the combined destructive firepower used cumulatively throughout the *whole* of human history. The UK's Trident nuclear armoury currently has around 200 warheads, the capacity of which amounts to 1,280 times that used at Hiroshima. By today's weapons standards, the bomb dropped on that city was *small*—and yet at least 140,000 people were killed as a result of it. Today, there are around 27,000 nuclear warheads in the world, which amounts to over *one million* times the destructive power that was used on Hiroshima. The power now exists to destroy all of human life many times over—as if more than once made any sense. Moreover, as well as the immediate localised impact, the effects of radiation from nuclear strikes would spread across space and time in an unmanageable way, and hence there could be no discrimination between civilian and military targets, between belligerent and peaceful countries, or between present and future generations. Finally, it almost goes without saying, the effects of their use would also irreparably damage the ecology of the planet.

Nuclear weapons have, unlike all previous armaments, the ability to effect not only human (and animal and plant) death on a massive scale, but also the unique potential to effect extinction. This is the 'universal death' that Einstein and Russell identified, and what Schell refers to as 'the second death':

in one sense, extinction is less terrible than death, since extinction can be avoided, while death is inevitable; but in another sense extinction is more terrible—is the more radical nothingness—because extinction ends death just as surely as it ends birth and life. Death is only death; extinction is the death of death.

(Schell, 1982, p 119)

I am concerned here with how the law engages with this. On one reading, the legalisation of nuclear weapons amounts to the legalisation of possible extinction. No matter how one defines the term, it is hard to imagine anything more profoundly irresponsible than this. On another reading, though, we might want to ask some more searching questions: for example, how is it *possible* to make sense of—and how is it possible to make *legal* sense of—the extreme violence and suffering that we know the use of nuclear weapons to entail? Is it not the case that we reach a limit of comprehension—and legal comprehension—here? How *can* we—and what does it mean to—measure, or try to provide a measure for, nuclear devastation? I will start by testing out these questions with reference to the question of the legality of nuclear weapons.

Legalising the disaster

In 1996, the International Court of Justice gave its Advisory Opinion on the following question put to it by the General Assembly of the United Nations: '*Is the threat or use of nuclear weapons in any circumstance permitted by international law?*' In brief, its response was the following (paragraph pinpoints in brackets): that the threat or use of nuclear weapons was neither explicitly authorised nor outlawed in international law; that all states had a right to self-defence, and that the tests of the threat or use of force were whether the action was necessary and proportionate to that defensive end [46]; that their threat or use operated within international law's regulation of the use of force under the United Nations Charter, as well as within the requirements of international humanitarian law; that there was an obligation to negotiate in good faith towards disarmament. Emphasising what was said a moment ago, the Court explicitly acknowledged the distinctiveness of nuclear weapons in these terms [35]: 'The destructive power of nuclear weapons cannot be contained in either space or time. They have the potential to destroy all civilization and the entire ecosystem of the planet.' This made it 'imperative for the Court to take account of the unique characteristics of nuclear weapons, and in particular their destructive capacity, their capacity to cause untold human suffering, and their ability to cause damage to generations to come' [36].

The Court concluded, by an 8:7 majority carried by the presiding judge's vote, that 'the threat or use of nuclear weapons would generally be contrary to the rules of international law applicable in armed conflict, and in

particular the principles and rules of international humanitarian law'
[105(2)E]. The latter rules emphasise the obligation to discriminate between
combatants and non-combatants, and the prohibition on causing 'unnecessary suffering' to combatants [78]. The Court found, therefore, that, 'In view
of the unique characteristics of nuclear weapons . . . the use of such weapons
in fact seems scarcely reconcilable with respect for such requirements' [95].
However, it continued, the Court 'does not have sufficient elements to enable
it to conclude with certainty that the use of nuclear weapons would necessarily be at variance with the principles and rules of law applicable in armed
conflict in any circumstance' [95] adding that the Court 'cannot lose sight of
the fundamental right of every State to survival, and thus its right to resort to
self-defence, in accordance with Article 51 of the [UN] Charter, when its
survival is at stake' [96]. The majority judgment was, therefore, that:

> in view of the current state of international law, and of the elements of
> fact at its disposal, the Court cannot conclude definitively whether the
> threat or use of nuclear weapons would be lawful or unlawful in an
> extreme circumstance of self-defence, in which the very survival of a
> State would be at stake.
>
> [105(2)E]

One interpretation of this Opinion is that it amounted to a political compromise, whereby a strong statement about the devastating effects of nuclear
weapons was made while, simultaneously, the loophole offered by the final
statement meant that nuclear powers could justifiably hold onto their
weapons. In essence, that is, the decision of the Court was, in fact, no decision; rather, the Court, in saying that it was unable to decide ('*the Court
cannot conclude definitively*'), declared *non liquet* (this was the view of the
majority opinions taken by Justices Higgins and Schwebel, who dissented).
This loophole—a loophole, according to some, the size of Armageddon—
was one in favour of which the nuclear powers had made a strong argument,
because it meant that nuclear 'business as usual' was legal. All it required was
that the nuclear powers make a sufficiently plausible case for saying that it
was not *necessarily* the case that, in any or all possible uses of nuclear
weapons, breach of either the laws relating to the use of force or of international humanitarian law would occur. The UK, for example, in its written
submission stated that, 'the question whether the use of a nuclear weapon
would be contrary to the principle of proportionality is not one which can be
answered in the abstract but only by reference to the circumstances of each
individual case' (Written Submission, para 3.71). A common example offered
for a proportionate use was the case of a 'small' nuclear strike against a
military submarine in the middle of an ocean, which, it was argued, would
have none of the devastating effects associated with the bombing of a city. In
other words, since it was not possible to determine in advance that a nuclear

strike was necessarily in breach of international law, any and each use of nuclear weapons could only be assessed *after their use* on a case-by-case basis to determine whether, in fact, it had been consistent with international law. This left it open to nuclear powers to argue that it was theoretically and practically possible that the use of such weapons would not breach the law, and, as such, the contemporary possession or threat of use of nuclear weapons was not in itself illegal. This position was maintained in the face of a range of opposing principles that could legally restrict a state's use of force, including those concerning the indiscriminate nature of nuclear strikes, environmental law obligations, respect for the neutrality of states and genocide. On the last mentioned, the Court itself argued that 'the prohibition of genocide would be pertinent in this case if the recourse to nuclear weapons did indeed entail the element of intent, towards a group as such, required by the provision [of the 1948 Genocide Convention]'. Whether wiping out a particular group of people would be found to be genocidal, however—and here we might reflect back on the discussion of intention in Part II of this chapter—would depend on a number of factors, pre-eminent among which would be the intention of the actor in destroying the population. A finding of genocide may therefore be excluded, because the same effects could, according to this logic, be carried out 'unintentionally'. Either way, 'In the view of the Court, it would only be possible to arrive at such a conclusion after having taken due account of the circumstances specific to each case' [26].

Of course, in practical terms, waiting for the effects of a nuclear strike—or series of strikes, including possible nuclear retaliation—to determine their legality or otherwise seems a rather risky, if not to say potentially futile, gesture. There may be nothing, and no one left, to make such a determination and, even if there were to be such a determination, in a post-nuclear strike world, the issue of legality—no doubt to be assessed through lengthy and detailed legal disputation and judgment—would most likely be a rather trivial one in the context of massive deaths, radiation contamination and the desperate attempts at survival of those left.

This was, in many respects, the stance taken by some of the dissenting judgments. Notably, Judge Weeramantry rejected outright the sophistries of the case-by-case approach, claiming that the threat or use of nuclear weapons was categorically prohibited in international law. According to Weeramantry, the 'euphemisms' to be found in the language of those who defended nuclear weapons—the 'disembodied language of military operations and the polite language of diplomacy'—'conceal the horror of nuclear war, diverting attention to intellectual concepts such as self-defence, reprisals, and proportionate damage which can have little relevance to a situation of total destruction' [II.2]. Such diversions, he argued, 'side-track the real issues of extermination by the million, incineration of the populations of cities, genetic deformities, inducement of cancers, destruction of the food chain, and the imperiling of civilization' [II.2]. The 'intellectual' and conceptual wordplay and legal niceties were, to Weeramantry, the juridical symptoms of what we have seen Schell identify as the '*insane calmness*': the calmness and insanity of those who philosophise with technical distinctions in the face of extinction.

But there was another kind of problem that, for Weeramantry, lay behind the majority Opinion. Where the Court's position failed to confirm the illegality of the threat or use of nuclear weapons, of necessity, it seemed to require an *engagement* with the '*horror*' that he, and so many others, identified with their use. Such an engagement, in law, was of a very specific type and involved a *calculation* (or set of calculations) in terms of the proportionality of military means to ends. But given the unique nature of the effects of nuclear weapons—as the majority Opinion had, in fact, recognised—then, Weeramantry argued, 'precise assessment of the nature of the appropriate and proportionate response by a nation stricken by a nuclear attack becomes *impossible*' [IV.2] (emphasis added). What was of significance in engaging with the possibility of *legal* assessment of the use of nuclear weapons (or, in fact, any massive deployment of force) was the necessity of 'speaking in terms of measurement—measurement of the intensity of the attack and the proportionality of the response'. And yet it was precisely this requirement that the law could not countenance in the case of nuclear weapons. As Weeramantry emphasised:

> one can measure only the measurable. With nuclear war, the quality of measurability ceases. Total devastation admits of no scales of measurement. We are in territory where the principle of proportionality becomes devoid of meaning.
>
> [IV.2]

Hence the effects of the use of nuclear weapons could not, for Weeramantry, be given measure by the law. In more conventional imagery, we might say that the consequences of their use were not something that could be put in the balance, or scales, of legal justice. One cannot 'calculate' with extinction. As Chimni expressed it (quoted by Weeramantry):

> The question is in fact one which cannot be legitimately addressed by law at all since it cannot tolerate an interpretation which negates its very essence. The end of law is a rational order of things, with survival as its core, whereas nuclear weapons eliminate all hopes of realising it. In this sense, nuclear weapons are unlawful by definition.
>
> [V.1]

This is a significant observation. What it points to, to put it in slightly different terms, is, at one level, a fundamental jurisprudential problem: if there is an internal relation between legal norms and force (or enforceability)—as is commonly assumed—then what happens when the legal norms are overwhelmed by the very means of their enforcement? The law, the very possibility of human law, could be extinguished by the use of force that nuclear weapons can deliver. Such categorical—not to say, human—collapse would make no sense in terms of *authorising* force. In this case, something has to give, and it is this, at least in part, that leads Weeramantry to see that only one conclusion is feasible: the finding that the majority supports, with its enormous loop-hole, must be categorically wrong as a matter of existing law. As such, the case *could*—and could only—be decided by choosing to declare illegal the threat or use of nuclear weapons. Only by declaring that their use is *never* permissible can the attempt to measure the immeasurable be avoided and the rationality of legal organisation be preserved. In other words, only by declaring their illegality—by recognising and then excluding the immeasurable from legal calculation—can the dangers inherent in the *non liquet* majority opinion be obviated.

Of course, this argument did not prevail and we will return to that fact in a moment. But there is another slightly different interpretation of the significance of the *non liquet* reading of the Opinion in which something more profound was arguably signalled, if not necessarily in a way in which the Court intended. According to this view, the immeasurable nature of the effects of the use of nuclear weapons registers only as something that cannot register at all, *even to be excluded*. This is an interpretation offered by Martii Koskenniemi (1997). He suggests that, 'In the legal argument about nuclear weapons, the enormity and exceptional character, indeed the *unthinkability* of the threatening wrong finds no signification and therefore cannot be taken into account' (Koskenniemi, 1997, p 155, emphasis in original). One way to understand the *non liquet* nature of the judgment would thus be to see it as a *symptom* of the unique and ungraspable enormity—the unthinkability—of the matter at hand. On this account, the conventional duty of a court to give judgment—that is, to declare the law and to decide one way on that basis—could not be fulfilled in this instance; rather, the undecidability expressed in the judgment, it might be said, mirrored the inexpressibility of harm, the 'untold' suffering, that the use of nuclear weapons would produce. This fact of the unimaginable, of the immeasurable that remains (and must remain) unmeasured, stuns the law: it stuns the law into the silence that is the extraordinary and exceptional judgment of non-judgment that is the *non liquet*.

According to Koskenniemi, what this case shows us are precisely the limits of legal reason: as he puts it, 'a purely rational, legal-technical approach to the massive killing of the innocent—the crux of the questions posed to the International Court of Justice—cannot be pursued without unacceptable moral and political consequences' (Koskenniemi, 1997, pp 137–8). Why? Because 'the legal reasoning available to the Court is unable to reach the core of the request—the massive killing of the innocent—and that to think otherwise would presume an image of international law, and of ourselves as international lawyers, we have good reason to reject' (1997, pp 140–1). The inability of the Court to decide whether the threat or use of nuclear weapons was 'in *any circumstance* permitted' (as the original question to which it was responding was formulated) was avoided because any rational engagement with it—either for *or* against—meant calculation had entered, and calculation here meant the commensurating, balancing and deciding that legal reasoning demands. But the limits of the law and legal reason were reached because it could make *no sense* to undertake this kind of balancing and decision here: that would require being willing, ultimately, to ask for more and more justifications, more and more *proof*—and hence open the way for more and more exceptions and qualifications—of why the massive killing of innocents is wrong. That question remained beyond the law, beyond reasoning, as only ever (if it is to be meaningful) self-evidencing: it is here, says Koskenniemi, that 'reason and justification refer away from themselves, into what is accepted outside as a matter of faith, and in particular to the social practices in which what we do is constitutive of what we are' (1997, p 157).

This *failure*, then, to take rational cognisance of that which is beyond reasoning or proof is what stuns the law into silence and avoids turning the unthinkable into its other. It is that very failure, in a sense, that is its success, because it is that which founds the *possibility* of legal regulation in community. Moreover, it also founds the possibility of moral or political engagement and critique. Where law determines, it can overdetermine, especially, says Koskenniemi, in so far as it would constitute a reliance on the authority of the legal response at the expense of personal engagement and judgement. And it is, he urges, in both of these respects, that the 'Court's silence . . . was a beneficial silence inasmuch as it, and only it, could leave room for the workings of the moral impulse, the irrational, non-foundational appeal against the killing of the innocent' (Koskenniemi, 1997, p 153).

I have a great deal of sympathy with the understandings offered by Weeramantry and Koskenniemi. But they do not, it seems to me, fully capture the nature and significance of the Opinion. There are two related points that suggest this. The first can be stated plainly: the Court *has* measured the immeasurable. While it is tempting to follow the suggestion that human suffering on a massive scale cannot be measured against the law or against reason, that measurement is precisely what the Court was able to do: such suffering *was* able to be reckoned with. The Court was willing to say that mass killing or environmental degradation, as a consequence of the use of nuclear weapons, were *factors* to be taken into account when assessing the proportionality of the use of nuclear weapons—but these factors had to be balanced up against others, most notably the right of the state to survival. Hence the Court decided that this suffering *did* form part of the analysis that could be carried out when applying its legal reasoning, in the course of interpreting and weighing up the merits of the different legal requirements.

And this, crucially and contrary to Koskenniemi's reading, does *not* signal the collapse of law's reason or the implosion of law's objective rationality; in fact, the reverse is true. It exemplifies—it *embodies*—law's reason. Even to the point of mass killing, to the point of possible genocide, even to the point of possible extinction, the law—its forms of legal reasoning, its techniques of measuring and weighing—does, and will be expected to, make that judgment. It is true that extinction may indeed be '*scarcely reconcilable*' with international humanitarian law, but it is only *after the event* that that judgment can finally be made. Up until that point, the use of nuclear weapons was potentially legal (or, at least technically, not yet necessarily illegal). Each case, as the UK representation urged, must be taken in its turn, even if that case was extinction (although we can be reasonably confident, of course, that the extinction of all human life consequent on a nuclear holocaust will have been illegal).

Let us note two things about the operation of legal reason briefly, in parenthesis, here. Firstly, the reasoning in this instance represents a grotesque instantiation of a technique that is all too familiar in legal reasoning. This was one identified by Jeremy Bentham (1792) as the principal mode of common law judging, which he referred to as '*dog-law*': if your dog does something you want it not to, you wait till it does it, *then* beat it. Secondly, there is a continuity—distant as it may seem from this case—with law's ordinary ability to measure what seems immeasurable. This can be found in what might appear to be the trivial sense in which, for example, the law of torts operates: so many pounds' compensation for the negligently caused loss of a leg; more for an eye; less for a finger, etc. The law has no trouble dealing with these apparent incommensurabilities. The ability to put a monetary value on non-economic suffering caused by a wrong inflicted on someone is standard practice. Of course, it can never be an exact equivalent and commonly payment is recognised as being inadequate compensation, and to some extent the sum is an acknowledgement of *that* fact. But still some reckoning, some equivalence or measurability, is not only deemed viable, but is the *modus operandi* of tort law. Moreover, it is an accepted and culturally dominant one in modernised Western societies. So, from the point of view of legal reasoning, this act of measurement and balancing as a necessary means of making a decision makes sense.

It is this path, not that of incommensurability, that has been taken here. That is what has been decided. But if this is the case, how are *we* to make sense of it, given our concern with law's role in the legitimation of suffering? It is perhaps tempting to downplay the legal reasoning aspect of it and understand it as merely a pragmatic set of manoeuvres on the way to justifying what is, in fact, the real reason for the decision: namely, a political compromise that seeks to acknowledge both the reality of the overwhelming political and military power of the nuclear states, and the desire to keep from jeopardy the very status of the court itself. Perhaps, alternatively, we might treat the legal reasoning aspects of the case as little more than an absurdity (and thus as something that should not be overanalysed), given that it has come up against the technological power of something uniquely and excessively destructive.

But to conclude in either of these ways would be to make a mistake at a number of levels. Firstly, the judgment and the judgment's reasoning are, in turn, reasoned *on* and *with*—by politicians, judges, lawyers, defendants and protesters—and, in this sense, it has very real effects. Consider two such effects, taken from different perspectives, in the following examples. On the one hand, the ICJ Opinion was recently cited, explored and agreed with in a Criminal Appeal Court judgment in Scotland, concerning the question of whether criminal activity carried out by protestors at the nuclear submarine base at Faslane on the river Clyde was legitimate, in so far as it aimed to try to stop the commission of a greater crime: namely, the threat of use of nuclear weapons. In a complex decision (based on a number of legal factors), the Appeal Court held that action such as those of the protestors was not legally warranted in Scotland. The Court stated, very much in line with the ICJ Opinion, that:

> We are not persuaded that even upon the respondants' description of, or hypothesis as to, the characteristics of Trident it would be possible to say *a priori* that a threat to use it, or its use, could never be seen as compatible with the requirements of international law.
>
> (Lord Advocate's Reference No 1 of 2000 [93])

In cases such as this, we are returned to the effects of the law's juridical architecture that we discussed earlier. In this particular case, we see that the law's authority claims that this decision is correct and whether or not it is just, reasonable or just plain crazy does not halt the reasoning from having consequences. In such cases, the reasoning of the ICJ Opinion impacts directly upon prosecutions, trials, people's criminal records and on the imposition of fines or imprisonment for those protesters who continue to oppose the possession of nuclear weapons.

Contiguously, and just as importantly, the judgment is relied upon to pursue continued nuclear policies at the political, military, economic and administrative levels, with all of the knock–on effects that this has, from questions of security and threats to it, to the impact on governmental spending priorities, and, ultimately, to an increased likelihood of nuclear proliferation and devastation occurring at some point. Thus the legal imprimatur —for all its postulated madness—operates with more or less direct effect in the material and institutional world, from local courts to the funding of billion-dollar death sciences. That legal stamp therefore provides a powerful legitimacy according to which the potential for large-scale human and environmental damage in the future is made thinkable.

None of this is fully captured by seeing the Opinion in the way that Koskenniemi suggests. That said, and in a way familiar from some of the analysis in this and the previous chapter, Koskenniemi does correctly identify how reliance on the law may be used as a diversionary mechanism, when it facilitates denials of responsibility that are grounded in legal authority and which result, as he succinctly puts it, in 'complicity with cruelty induced by passive faith in authority' (1997, p 159). But it is in exactly this sense that the judgment leaves its mark on morality, just as it leaves its mark on political and military practice, because it already circumscribes these spaces and, indeed, it already striates the very texture of what it finds there. This is not to say that it fully determines moral or political responses, particularly critical ones. But, in line with the processes we associated with both the 'management of morality' and law's influence beyond the reach of its regulatory boundary, it would be folly to understand such responses as separate from, or prior to, the powerful institutional and highly meditated world within which they exist: the world we identified already as that of political, military, economic and administrative logics, the world chock-full of nuclear weapons, all of which are bolstered by the fact and reasoning of the ICJ's Opinion.

And this leads us to the second point, which concerns the role of the state. As a sovereign entity and the subject of international law, the state—or more precisely, in this instance, the state's *right* to self-defence—is the linchpin on which the supposed exception in paragraph 105(2)E of the Opinion is founded. It is this right of the state, and only the state, that holds out the possibility that nuclear weapons may be used lawfully. This right is perhaps the only thing of a truly absolute nature here, since it is the 'fundamental right of every State to survival'.

In realising the significance of this, we might add a corrective, or perhaps a change in emphasis, to a point that Michel Foucault (1990) makes in respect of this issue. Writing of a transformation from the early modern to the present eras, Foucault suggests that:

> Wars are no longer waged in the name of a sovereign who must be defended; they are waged on behalf of the existence of everyone; entire populations are mobilized for the purpose of wholesale slaughter in the name of life necessity: massacres have become vital . . . The atomic situation is now at the end point of this process: the power to expose a whole population to death is the underside of the power to guarantee an individual's continued existence . . . the existence in question is no longer the juridical existence of sovereignty; at stake is the biological existence of a population. If genocide is the dream of modern powers, this is not because of a recent return of the ancient right to kill; it is because power is situated and exercised at the level of life, the species, the race, and the large-scale phenomenon of population.
>
> (Foucault, 1990, p 137)

Foucault is correct in observing the threats that modernity's *'achievements'* represent, and the ways in which bio-politics and population figure in this. But in light of the ICJ Opinion, we might suggest that he has underplayed the way in which the juridical realm, in its relation to the sovereignty of the modern state, still plays a profoundly important role in assessing the ways in which 'massacres' will be legitimated. The reason for acknowledging the centrality of the juridical realm here refers back to an earlier observation: in terms of juridical discourse, reference cannot be made directly to populations or biological existence, but only to legal phenomena. Only legal norms can be breached, not forms of life or species or whatever. The 'biological existence of a population' may well be at stake—and this is nowhere more obvious than in the case of nuclear weapons—but it remains the case that it is still the *sovereign*, the *right* of the sovereign state, that must be defended and it is where, and only where, *it* is threatened that massacres may ensue. Foucault claims that we should 'not be deceived' by the 'clamorous legislative activity' that the Enlightenment brought with it, since these codes 'were the forms that made an essentially normalizing power possible' (1990, p 144). But is it not, in fact, the *inverse* of this that remains true: that, to paraphrase, we should not be deceived by the normalising power of disciplines or bio-politics, because it is rather these that are the forms which make an essentially *juridical* power acceptable? It may be that biological life has appeared on the political scene in modernity in a new way, but it is still the 'juridical existence of the sovereign' that *is* ultimately central to the production of suffering of this worst possible kind.

It might be countered, however (although not by Foucault), that populations or species life find their instantiation in the juridical realm through the medium of the state and, in this sense, that the former are given legal protection through their representation in the latter. But to argue in this way would be to make an important error, because there is a crucial disjunction between lives and populations—or, put more plainly, the lives of people as citizens—and the juridical form of the state, and it consists centrally in this: that the people may suffer harms, but only the state will suffer a wrong. In international law, the protection of the state is not equivalent to the protection of its people. And *that* is why people may be destroyed—in the name of the state.

In his realisation of this, Schell (1982, p 218) had urged us to confront the fact that it is 'National sovereignty [that] lies at the very core of the political issues that the peril of extinction forces upon us'. The Opinion confirms this, but it refuses to do other than normatively endorse it. In the next chapter, we will look to some of the significations of this in terms of citizenship and complicity. But we must take note now that for all of the—sometimes no doubt relevant—discussion of the changing nature of the state under conditions of political and economic globalisation, as well as all of the importance of recognising the distinctiveness of disciplinary power and bio-politics, in this instance—and this instance is, of course, a highly concerning one—it is clear that we are very far from being 'beyond the sovereign state'. The right of states to use nuclear weapons in self-defence under 'extreme circumstances' testifies to the power that this institution, practically and in thought, retains. And in this sense it reminds us directly of the fact that it is, perhaps more than any other factor, legal *right* that is capable of legitimating the extensive commission of suffering of innocents.

We should never forget that it will be innocents who will suffer most extensively, not only because there are more of them, but because those most responsible for (or least innocent of) causing the harms—namely politicians, civil servants and the military elites—will, holed up in their bunkers, be least likely to be directly affected. Those with least say in the whole destructive process, in other words, will bear the brunt of its effects. And this, rather than being exceptional, is merely a continuation of the trend in modernity that has seen the increasing democratisation of death in political violence, one in which civilian casualties have risen from 5 to 90 per cent of those killed in military conflicts in the course of the twentieth century, the most violent in all human history. Such would appear to be the trajectory of modern democratic 'participation': a legally organised means of justifying, or at least excusing, the deployment of mass violence by some in the name of the state, with all of the corresponding and extensive devastation and suffering of innocents that this entails.

Hence the state's constituted power—its legal authority and right— involves the ultimate in *de*-constituting power, which is the power that nuclear weapons represents to us all. As Asad puts it, it means that:

> the manufacture, possession, and deployment of weapons of mass destruction (chemical, nuclear, and biological) must be counted as instances of declared governmental readiness to engage in 'cruel, inhuman and degrading treatment' against civilian populations even when they are not actually used.
>
> (Asad, 1996, p 1097)

And it is this willingness to deploy 'cruel modern technologies of destruction [which] are integral to modern warfare' that means that 'In war, the modern state demands from its citizens not only that they kill and maim others, but also that they themselves suffer cruel pain and death' (ibid). This suffering, moreover, will not only *not* register as injury, but, because it is according to the nature of legal norms and doctrine, it is what the law demands and thus *expects*. It cannot be emphasised enough that this is the legal position that the ICJ and all of its followers, in the seats of national parliaments, courts and political parties, endorse. In this respect, the mode of reasoning employed by the court and by those who rely on its dicta, must, as Schell observes, 'in all honesty admit that their scheme contemplates the extinction of man in the name of protecting national sovereignty' (1982, p 218).

There is one last point to be made in closing this section. I have suggested, for a number of reasons, that it is important to accept the Opinion of the ICJ as one that has very real and potentially awful consequences, in policies, legal practices and international politics, and in how they are brought to bear on the commission of human suffering. Understanding the Opinion as a non-decision tends to underplay that continuity. I have suggested, instead, that law's reason does indeed see itself as being able to measure the immeasurable, even in the most extreme possible scenarios. We should not shy away from this by making some assertion about law's inadequacies or limits. The final, and I think the most important, reason why not is this: that failure to do this, failure to understand this *as* the reality, would not do justice to those for whom legally organised mass killing has *already been a reality*.

Taking seriously *that* suffering means being constantly reminded that the law's ability to legitimate the delivery of extensive suffering is, and will likely continue to be, part of the tradition of modern Western law. But where technological advancement has now outstripped all previous forms, where scientific knowledge has produced a destructive capacity that results in a uniquely powerful and potentially ultimately devastating situation, then the continuity of that tradition *does*, now and for the first time, face a potentially overwhelming challenge. Science thus makes a provocation to law in a novel way and one that means, not to put too fine a point on it, that there is something of a race on when it comes to law's relation to nuclear capability. That race finds its expression in a new understanding of the old medieval maxim, a maxim that seems now like nothing short of a chilling wager: let justice be done, though the world perish.

Chapter 4

Complicity in organised irresponsibility

Asad's (1996) observation that the modern state, through its legal norms and institutions, demands of its citizens '*not only that they kill and maim others, but also that they themselves suffer cruel pain and death*' provides a cruel but vital jolt that prompts us to consider further the relationship of law to its citizens. Are citizens themselves implicated in the acts of their government? Are they in any sense responsible for these acts? In the immediate context of a discussion of the potentially apocalyptic effect of the use of nuclear weapons, it does seem that it would be a strange phenomenon that would see such responsibility as signifying nothing less than a mass suicide pact. And yet is this not, in actual fact, where we really are, right now: towards the end point of a modern tradition in which what was once thought of as a highly valued achievement of the modern ideals of the state—*consent* to being governed—must now, in tandem with technological capabilities, be best understood as having been grotesquely deformed, the social compact having become the suicide pact? Unless we desire to keep a sense of denial functionally and perilously intact, is this not what the reality of the culmination of full citizen participation is now likely to mean? And if participation is not complete, if it is not us, then it will be—according to the colonial logic—others who die, and so we are either masochists or sadists, or victims. Can that be correct? Did Nietzsche (1972, s 156) turn out to be right in precisely this respect when he observed that while 'Madness is something rare in individuals . . . in groups, parties, people, ages it is the rule'?

If this is not correct, then it is *not* because the reality of danger is different from the description just offered. (The nuclear and environment hazards cannot be wished away by ignoring them.) It surely must be largely because there is a decisive sense in which the acts of government, for all of the current claims to democratic legitimacy, still cannot be other than alienated from the responsibility of citizens. And yet, despite this, in a democratic polity, there would seem, at least at some level, to be a desirability in claiming that the people *do* bear some responsibility for the acts of their governments, if not least because they have participated in their constitution, funding or election.

Such issues have a great political heritage and baggage that come with them. Answers to questions such as these are contested in all kinds of ways and it is not my intention to review these here; rather, my task is a narrower one. In line with the analysis of the book, it is to try to understand what role law and legal institutions might play in so far as they may be thought to organise irresponsibility. This is the aim of this chapter. In order to give it focus, I will concentrate on a case study that, I hope, gives a sense of these greater concerns, but does so in a more detailed way according to which we can gain an insight into what work legal roles do in the context of citizens' responsibilities and irresponsibilities. The case study returns us to Iraq, but brings our attention to more recent developments than those we considered in Chapter 1.

'Not in our name'?

One of the striking features of the period of sanctions against Iraq was how little their devastating effects registered on the sensibilities of the citizens of those countries imposing them. Certainly in Britain—I will use this as my reference point here—and despite many determined efforts to have the issue made persistently and more publicly prominent, there was, and still is, little awareness of, or activity around, the question of the government's—far less, British citizens'—complicity in mass deaths. No doubt an important part of the explanation for this must include the nature of the legality of the enterprise at which we looked in detail in the first chapter. But in respect of Iraq, that situation changed with the British and American proposal to invade the country in early 2003. This proposal, and its subsequent actualisation in March 2003, produced an immense reaction by way of denunciation both by other governments and in widespread protests by many people throughout the world, including unprecedented demonstrations against it in Britain.

Although the invasion was itself illegal, as seems to be the general consensus among international lawyers (Sands, 2006, ch 8; Gazzini, 2005), I am less concerned with this given that my focus here is on the effects of legal activities in the legitimation of human suffering. This is not to say, of course, that I would want to ignore the fact that the invasion was, and remains, a human and political disaster. But as a serious breach of international law, the main perpetrators in governmental hierarchies—starting with George W Bush and Tony Blair—ought to be brought to trial for, at the very least, crimes of aggression. So my intention is not to discuss that here, but to analyse instead what the existence this time of widespread citizen opposition to the invasion can tell us about the nature of how law organises *citizens'* irresponsibility in the legitimation of suffering.

What is perhaps most interesting, generally and specifically in respect of the themes of this book, about the nature of the protests against the invasion is that they took the form of a *disavowal* of implication in the actions of government. Of the most prominent banners on the day of mass protests against the proposed invasion were those that stated simply '*Not in our name*' or, for the less solidaristic, '*Not in my name*'. Here was an explicit statement of withdrawal from a potential complicity with the proposed actions of the government and an attempt to disconnect those actions—that were thought, rightly as it turned out, likely to result in the large-scale deaths and injuries of Iraqi citizens—with the personal beliefs or consciences of the citizens.

On one reading, this form of protest might be seen as part of an important lineage, one that involved determined dissent against government injustice. In this instance, the mass protests were a demonstration of genuine outrage at, and rejection of, the unjustified and devastating violence to be unleashed against Iraqi people. The protests were a rejection of association with what was argued to be little more than imperial greed, and they accordingly abjured senseless violence and a raising of the global insecurity stakes. As such, they signified an intentional disavowal of responsibility on behalf of citizens vis à vis their government: this is not our doing, it is yours, and our consciences will not be sullied by your brutality and misjudgement.

But how successful could this withdrawal be? Was there not, in fact, some-thing else, something more unsettling about this sentiment? The uneasiness here derived from the fact that *this* disavowal seemed too *easy*. Somehow it failed to match up to the powers, not simply of the state, but of the complex reality of more or less formalised institutional settings within which people are and act—the complex divisions of labour in our intellectual, material and mediated lives that we considered in Chapter 2—which, all together, make the notion of a singular and simple moral *disavowal* of the state's action so profoundly problematic. In fact, was it not all of these very same diversifying concepts and institutional practices that had helped neutralise outrage and *distance* the sense of complicity during the killing years of sanctions against Iraq? Was it not, in other words, precisely the *complexity* of the situation—international politics, global finance, the minutiae of sanctions lists and UN resolutions, oil prices, media coverage, and so on—that made it easier to see, in that case, *no* connections between 'our' moral thought, 'our' name and dead Iraqis?

If 'our' private consciences were not devastated, or even overly troubled, by the destruction caused by a legally enacted sanctions regime, it was because they could be absolved through the *disaggregation of responsibility* effected in the context of complex causes and distant effects, a significant element in the make-up of which was their very legality. But if this were so, why would 'our' withdrawal of our name be any more relevant or efficacious now? Moreover, what grounds would there be for claiming an exception to what might appear otherwise to be some continuing *implication* in our government's acts, through paying taxes or participation in voting? Wouldn't this amount to no more than Stanley Milgram's assessment of the 'so-called intellectual resist-ance' (1974, p 10) in occupied Europe during World War II: '. . . merely indulgence in a consoling psychological mechanism?'

A whole series of troubling questions might then be asked about the nature of this citizen disavowal: who—or what?—was best to judge which actions were and were not in 'our' name? Were 'we' best placed to judge this, best able to decide when 'we' could move in and out of positions of responsibility? (What responsibility? Responsibility for what?) Or was it, in fact, *not* ourselves that could best judge this, but rather some other persons or institutions: 'our' representative, our democratically elected government? Or perhaps some court somewhere? Or the United Nations? Or, indeed, the Iraqis themselves? And besides, was it not conceivable that 'our' involvement was, in fact, *heightened* the more our democratically elected government strained its legal mandate? And if this were so, what else remained—remains—to be done beyond a statement of disavowal?

These are provocative and complex questions that cannot all be answered here. Rather, I want to use them, as I have suggested, as a springboard for reflecting on the general themes of the book and for considering specifically whether, and to what extent, the *legal* aspects of the citizen's role *over*determine the attempted protests of disavowal. If the latter were so, it would happen in a very curious way and with an unexpected implication: that is, the legal influence could overdetermine the meaning of the protest, but it would do so in a way that nonetheless led to a confirmation of the citizens' lack of responsibility, or rather, in terms we have been using here, to a disappearance of their responsibility among the norms of responsibility. In a way that needs to be brought out more explicitly, then, law's role here would foster an instance of organised irresponsibility of citizens.

It is to this issue that I now want to turn. In order to do this, it will be necessary to return to, and draw on, some of the key elements of the analysis developed in the preceding chapters. In particular, this will involve a fuller consideration of what, at the end of Chapter 2, I called 'responsibility transference'. But I will now consider this, along with several other features, specifically with regard to the techniques and implications of its legal manifestations.

Death and taxes

At the very end of her book on the Eichmann trial, Hannah Arendt (1977, p 279) declared forthrightly that 'politics is not like the nursery; in politics obedience and support are the same'. But is the same true for law? That is, when it comes to the production of harms, is 'our' involvement through obedience to law or the legal order not 'like the nursery' either? To paraphrase Arendt, *in law*, are obedience and support the same? If this were the case, then where law formally organises citizens' responsibilities and obligations, to the extent that these responsibilities and obligations are met, then law may also organise their *irresponsibility* in ways in which political or moral protest fails sufficiently to match up. In other words, if citizens are law-abiding, then they are co-opted not only juridically, but morally and politically, and obedience, however achieved or justified, equals support.

To pursue this possibility, consider the following view outlined in a letter to a British newspaper in 2004:

> I am troubled by the current vilification of Palestine suicide bombers. I have relatively more respect for a suicide bomber who, in killing a number of civilians, does at least sacrifice his own life than I have for an airman bomber who kills hundreds more civilians at the comparative safety of 20,000 feet.
>
> I am also troubled by the common prefix of 'innocent' before the word 'civilian'. If a civilian instructs and pays, through his taxes, others to kill his enemies on his behalf, I really don't think the term 'innocent' can be applied to him. I lived through the Blitz when it would never have occurred to either myself or any of my friends to have called ourselves 'innocent' and thereby have distinguished ourselves from our fighting men. We were all in the war together and privileged to share their dangers. Besides, when it came to killing 'innocent' civilians hardly anyone then decried the bombing of Dresden or Hiroshima.
>
> (Harper, 2004, p 13)

Memorably, another protest banner had said 'No taxation without representation', one of the rallying cries of the revolutionaries in the British colonies in North America in the eighteenth century. But does it not also have a *converse* signification? There can be no taxation *without* representation: there is no taxation without being represented. It appears that this is the understanding of the letter writer: taxpayers cannot help but be represented in the act of paying their taxes and this makes them all, with regard to their state's involvement in military action, say, at the very least 'Not innocent'.

There are a number of claims here, but the one with which I am primarily concerned is that of taxation. Consider two related sets of questions. First, is it the case that their payment of taxation makes taxpayers complicit in the acts of their state? When, as a matter of ordinary criminal law, someone pays for another to kill a person this counts as participation in murder: does that analogy hold in respect of taxation? According to the conventional wisdom, it does not hold and, in this respect, it conforms to the logic of compartmentalisation in legal categories to which we drew attention in Chapter 3: what appears as illegal under one legal description appears as legal under another and responsibility for harm does not transfer across the boundary. And yet, we might still want to ask, why shouldn't this analogy hold here, particularly when we are potentially dealing with harms on a massive scale? The answer is instructive and, as we shall see in a moment, it is one that is strongly rejected by some.

The second set of questions concerns the issue of 'innocent civilians'. If taxpayers contribute to the general fund out of which military action is paid for, do they not thereby 'share in the dangers' that may result from it? Do they not become legitimate targets or at least—as the civilians in the target country do—liable to being 'collateral damage' in any military response? Why *wouldn't* they? Questions of this sort are of very real import and there will be much disagreement over the answers to them. But I will not consider them further here, except to point this out: from the perspective of those causing harm to civilians, intention to target them (or rather the lack of such intention), and the necessity and proportionality of means to the ends of the military action, are the key measures according to which the commission of civilian suffering is designated legitimate. And yet such legal measures, as we have already seen, may cover a vast range of harms. Again, as Asad (1996, p 1097) forcefully expresses it: 'Given the aim of ultimate victory, the notion of "military necessity" can be extended indefinitely. Any measure that is intended as a contribution to that aim, no matter how much suffering it creates, may be justified in terms of "military necessity".' Because it is not the suffering itself that provides the measure, it is open to a great deal of ideological and institutional (and perhaps also media) power in determining the legal significance of the intention, proportionality and necessity in respect of the suffering caused. We have seen several instances of that now, but it has one obvious implication that needs to be emphasised in this context: from the point of view of any citizens, the law's power of definition to obliterate responsibility for harms *does* make citizens liable to becoming 'collateral damage'. And moreover, this much is clear: no amount of citizen disavowal will make each any less a target than any other citizen. As Rousseau (1973, p 208) expressed the situation generally, 'the citizen is no longer the judge of the dangers to which the law desires him to expose himself'.

Be that as it may, let us return to the first set of questions about complicity through taxation. In *Boughton v HM Treasury* [2006], recently decided in the English Court of Appeal, a protest group committed to pacifism—known as the Peace Tax Seven—raised a defence to withholding a portion of their taxes—they estimated around 10 per cent—that would go to military expenditure (including to the war in Iraq), claiming that, under the freedom of conscience guarantee of Art 9 of the European Convention on Human Rights, protection of their conscientious beliefs gave them legal entitlement to do so. The appellants noted that they were perfectly willing to pay their taxes—in full—but claimed that they should be able to pay a specified amount into a separate 'peace fund' in order that their Art 9 right not be breached. Their claim included the following arguments. Paying taxation for military expenditure is equivalent to fighting in a war, since usually—and according to well-established principles of criminal law—paying someone to kill or make preparations to kill for you is illegal. Moreover, where wars are now fought not with conscripts, but by professional soldiers using high-tech means, the long-standing right to conscientious objection should apply analogously to what amounted otherwise to 'financial conscription' in the commission of violence. As pacifists, complicity in killing in a war was contrary to their deeply held conscientious beliefs and so the exercise of their right to freedom of conscience is interfered with in the public realm to the extent that the government forces them to participate in the commission of violence through payment of taxes. Since freedom of conscience is a right protected by Art 9 of the Convention as incorporated into UK law, it is infringed by current taxation mechanisms, which afford them no opportunity to pay into an alternative non-military fund.

Their campaign—political as well as legal, and now destined for a hearing at the European Court of Human Rights—was supported by a number of MPs, MEPs and MSPs from a range of political parties (see www. peacetaxseven.com). The Treasury, unsurprisingly, rejected their arguments. The essence of its rejection, for reasons upheld on appeal, lay in reliance on *C v United Kingdom*, a 1983 decision of the European Commission of Human Rights, which was quoted in the Court of Appeal as follows (at [16]):

Article 9 primarily protects the sphere of personal beliefs and religious creeds, ie, the area which is sometimes called the forum internum. In addition, it protects acts which are intimately linked to these attitudes, such as acts of worship or devotion which are aspects of the practice of a religion or belief in a generally recognised form.

However, in protecting this personal sphere, Article 9 of the Convention does not always guarantee the right to behave in the public sphere in a way which is dictated by such a belief:- for instance, by refusing to pay certain taxes because part of the revenue so raised may be applied for military expenditure . . .

The obligation to pay taxes is a general one which has no specific conscientious implications in itself. Its neutrality in this sense is also illustrated by the fact that no tax payer can influence or determine the purpose for which his or her contributions are applied, once they are collected. Furthermore, the power of taxation is expressly recognised by the Convention system and is ascribed to the State by Article 1, First Protocol.

It follows that Article 9 does not confer on the applicant the right to refuse, on the basis of his convictions, to abide by legislation, the operation of which is provided for by the Convention, and which applies neutrally and generally in the public sphere, without impinging on the freedoms guaranteed by Article 9.

In ways that we will now explore, it is through the simultaneous combination and separation of different social systems that the defendants' claims are rebutted and their right to freedom of conscience held not to be breached. And it is in this respect that individual responsibility vanishes through intricate justificatory and institutional forms of what we might call systemic alchemy, central to which is the resilience of the modern state form and its law. Let us look more closely at how this works.

Taxation, a legal obligation, once paid, disappears from the radar of economic, political and moral accountability from the taxpayers' perspective: '*no tax payer can influence or determine the purpose for which his or her contributions are applied, once they are collected.*' The logic here is worth spelling out. According to the Treasury's reasoning (as recorded in the Court of Appeal judgment by Mummery LJ, at [32]):

> The position is that the taxes paid by the applicants are not in any real sense being used for military purposes. The tax paid is money received into the Consolidated Fund. It loses its separate identity. Amounts released from the Consolidated Fund or transferred into the National Loans Fund cannot be identified with the amounts of tax paid by the applicants.

Unlike in the criminal law scenario of paying a hit man to kill for you, money in the form of taxes retains no connection or trace of identity to its source. But, of course, this approach taken by the courts and the Treasury has a curious corollary: that *no one* pays for military expenditure. That is, if the applicants' taxes 'are not in any real sense being used for military purposes', and if these applicants are in no sense different from anyone else, then *any* individual person's taxes 'are not in any real sense being used for military purposes'. This apparent absurdity—that no taxpayer pays for something that is paid for by taxes—is explainable conceptually through a distinction between citizens as individual taxpayers and citizens as collectively represented in the singular form of the state. Thus the constituted state authority is representative of 'everyone', not 'every one'; it represents no one person (or group or moral persuasion) in particular—each becomes, in a sense, *anonymous*—but rather everyone 'neutrally and generally'. Thus no one in particular pays for anything in particular paid for by taxes, even though every *one* pays. This is the economic alchemy of the 'general will', as manifested in the constituted authority of the state: 'everyone' and no one pays for what is spent by taxation.

But the problem is, of course, that the living taxpayer *is* identifiable and *has* a name, known both to themselves and the Treasury. And here now is the legal alchemy: from the point of view of the taxation system, as understood and defined by the law, the legal obligation to pay an economic debt connects *directly* with personal identity at the point of payment (after all, it is the tax debtor that is personally liable to sanction for *non*-payment); yet the same legal system actively and simultaneously *disconnects* personal identity—and this is the crucial point—from *its own* moral understanding and obligation at the same—and any subsequent—point.

The question of perspective is pivotal here. From the legal perspective, the law decides 'the obligation to pay taxes . . . has no specific conscientious implications in itself'. The law would, so to speak, launder both the money and the moral conscience. From the point of view of the pacifists, however, the law *does* organise their responsibility and hence, in that specific sense, their personal culpability. It does so because, from their perspective and *despite* their political and moral opposition, when it comes to something that really counts in the production of harms (money for munitions that goes towards killing), the state *can and does* conscript the taxpayer in ways about which the objector can do nothing. For the objector, the economic connection directly links to moral culpability, despite the law's claim to sever it. The money raised and spent—and hence the actions of the state itself—cannot be otherwise than in the name of the objector. This is not, they point out, simply a matter of political preference being negated: it is a matter of complicity in killing through actions that nobody doubts is harmful to innocents. Thus when it comes to the law of the state—its conceptual and material underpinnings, and its societal dominance—*it* succeeds in defining the meaning of the moral problem, given that it demands the taxation be paid. And it does so in such a way that its actions and demands disallow alternative understandings of even 'private' conscience, because these are held in law to fail to transfer their meaning to the public realm: as the Court said, Art 9 'does not always guarantee the right to behave in the public sphere in a way which is dictated by such beliefs'.

This is why, when the state is involved, its legitimating and legal apparatuses—taxation law, criminal law, even human rights law—set the terms of engagement and moral understanding to certain limited and predetermined forms. From a cultural perspective, this relies on a deeply embedded belief that the actions of the state are qualitatively different from 'ordinary' acts. But from the pacifists' perspective, as mediated through legal, economic and political forms and their interrelation, it ensures the inevitability of complicity in killing. Put otherwise, this is the legal organisation of moral irresponsibility.

It might be objected that one cannot, or should not, be held responsible for something one could not otherwise have done. But this is precisely how irresponsibility is organised here. First, the sense of personal responsibility felt by the protestors—and who is to decide if they are *wrong* about this?— means that they do remain directly implicated as long as the current situation continues. So while, for the protestors, responsibility cannot be easily disavowed, the law of the state directs them to believe that payment of taxes for killing in military action has '*no specific conscientious implications in itself*'. Yet recalling Arendt's terms (1997), for the protestors obedience and support *are* the same. Protesting '*Not in our name*' while paying money towards the war effort cannot get one off the hook; the legally sanctioned *economic* contribution *dictates* personal responsibility. But that is not the legal position—and it is the legal position, due largely to the three features of the juridical architecture we have identified, that dominates. Thus, for the law, the only legitimate dissent will consist in allowing the protesters to claim that 'payment of their taxes in full without segregation is by compulsion, under protest and against their strongly held religious beliefs and consciences' (*Boughton* at [41]). But even this is too little and too much: on the one hand, for reasons explained, it is still insufficient, from the protestors' perspective, to negate complicity; on the other, according to the strict logic of taxation noted above, it is, from the legal perspective, unnecessary because taxation has 'no specific conscientious implications in itself'. In either case, however, we have a clear instance of the legal role of taxpayer determining the responsibility, and irresponsibility, of the person.

And this leads to a second point, which suggests something more profound, beyond even the protestors' position: that isolating responsibility as a straightforward question of personal responsibility fails to capture the complex ways in which our social systems and the concepts or expectations that support them actually operate. In this sense, the problem of '*Not in our name*' is an instance of a more general problematic we have seen throughout this book: that our basic concepts and categories, and the material and institutional practices within which they exist and make sense, are *simultaneously* ways of both asserting *and* deferring something—the argument, the obligation, the action or the silence, as these are given various meanings across the logics and roles of different social systems. Where responsibility in modern society has, indeed, become '*free-floating*', at least in so far as we understand this under sociological conditions that work to facilitate the dispersals of responsibility and the '*management of morality*', then attempting to establish or distinguish personal and legal obligations *simpliciter* provides only a superficial understanding of social action. The 'achievements' of modern society rely, as we have seen, on a number of institutional and technical forms through which action and its understanding are co-ordinated, but which concurrently allow for the proliferation of normative manipulations, connections and disconnections, which enable a splintering of normative meaning through which responsibilities are dispersed.

Perhaps the most important consequence of this can now be recognised for what it is, since it refers us back to our opening asymmetry. That is, while smaller scale actions that produce harms tend to be readily measurable in terms of their being breaches of the law, larger scale actions, with far *greater* harmful consequences, are not so readily measured. Responsibility is 'disappeared' variously through combinations, blockages and transferences that rely on, and perpetuate, the achievements of modern social structures and their role responsibilities. And, of course, this is nowhere more decisively achieved than where the measure of responsibility is precisely that which fails to allow responsibility for the production of harms to register at all; that is, where that measure is the law itself—where the harms are legal. Here, Hobbes's analysis (1996) retains its resilience down the centuries: that those actions that are legal can cause damage, but no injury, and that those who follow the law remain guiltless.

In coming towards our conclusion and in order to bring together these insights, we might recall again now what Bauman (1989, p 199) saw as being at the pinnacle of what he called society's '*morality-eroding mechanisms*': namely, 'the principle of sovereignty of state powers usurping supreme ethical authority on behalf of societies they rule'. We have seen in any number of instances—from ongoing colonial effects, to the contemporary scene of bloody invasions and the organisation of citizens' (ir)responsibilities—how important this is in the legitimation of human suffering. Under such circumstances, norms of responsibility cannot be thought apart from their social locations in diverse institutions, roles and technological forms (including, as we have seen, legal institutions, roles and forms), places in which personal responsibility and 'morality' may be deployed, disaggregated, neglected, disfigured, engaged and disengaged across a range of responsibility practices, and forms of knowledge and action. Such forms and processes cannot easily be rendered reducible to straightforward moral or political accounting. In fact, the practical and academic, or theoretical, tendency to think and act as if they *can* arguably itself constitutes an element in the operation of this aspect of the organisation of irresponsibility. Such a tendency commonly pays insufficient attention to the ways in which social action is so mediated and thus displays a failure fully to grapple with the how harms are produced.

The banner protesting '*Not in our name*' can arguably be read as a symptom of precisely this problematic. While the state and its law colonise meaning relentlessly through forms of legal validity and the general will, and through economic resources in the taxation system, the banner's ineffable protest symbolises, however inadequately, both the dispersal and evaporation of responsibilities, and the limitations of modern forms of representation and democracy to address it. But it also, in its inadequacy, shows how the law is left intact as the socially dominant and effective measure of what will be legitimate; and it shows how, consequently, the law plays a central role in the commission and production of suffering.

The protestors' enervated attempt, perhaps ultimately unsuccessful, to escape the overdetermination of institutional co-option therefore signifies *both* that the link between harms suffered and responsibility for causing them is all too easily severed, *and* that that severing is legitimated while all the while the production of suffering is paid for and hence goes on. The banner stands as a mark of how, in the legitimation of such suffering, the asymmetry between citizen and state is grotesquely reproduced and legitimated in the alchemies of our social systems, which, whether through the form of sanctions or governmental invasions, simultaneously mediate, prioritise and disconnect responsibilities in a play of disavowals that seem both comprehensible and yet deeply disturbing. From the perspective of those who suffer the harms, it explains what is at once an unmediated directness *and* the disappearance of responsibility for it of which the structures of organised irresponsibility are capable. There is, perhaps, no better encapsulation of this than that grasped in John Berger's (2003) observation that, 'it happens in their lives that people suffer from wrongs which are classified in separate categories; [yet they] suffer them simultaneously and inseparably'.

Law and the slaughterhouse

In this way, we come to a corollary of our general focus on the production and legitimation of suffering which are dependent on legal and not illegal processes. With the above analysis of the question of citizens' complicity in mind, we see that, rather than focusing on the perspective of disobedience or the disobedient, when it comes to the large-scale commission of harms we must consider instead, and increasingly, the more troubling perspective according to which, as Dwight Macdonald suggested, we must 'fear the person who obeys the law more than the one who disobeys it' (Bauman, 1989, p 151). Disavowing responsibility for harmful actions may be too easy when, from other perspectives—and specifically, as we have seen, from the economic and the legal, or some combination of the two—the complicitous irresponsibility that comes with law abidance is already assured. In such, potentially apocalyptic, scenarios, it is important that the tax bills have been paid.

Returning for a final time to our case studies, it is a perverse and deadly irony that the excuse for invading Iraq in 2003 was a fear of the spread of 'weapons of mass destruction'—because what could be more irresponsible than allowing a state's capability to be developed in ways that would threaten to destroy indiscriminately vast amounts of human, animal and plant life on the planet? What indeed, except perhaps this: the organisation of this very capability globally and legally. That, of course, is where we now are, with the nuclear state powers—several of whom who sit most prominently, and without irony, as defenders of world peace and security on the United Nations Security Council—shielding, as we have seen, their abominable weapons through the imprimatur of the legal right to possess, threaten and, in extreme circumstances, use nuclear weapons. Here, surely, we have reached the pinnacle of legally organised irresponsibility. And what, more than anything, is most telling about the situation is that it has become, following Arendt, so terribly, terrifyingly normal.

But perhaps in the end, like our observations in the opening chapter, this should not surprise us so much. As Sven Linqvist (2002) noted, it is not—or it should not be—knowledge that is lacking. In the same year as Eichmann was being tried and sentenced to death in Jerusalem, the legal philosopher HLA Hart published a book that confirmed his reputation as the pre-eminent

English-speaking jurist of the twentieth century. Among the many conceptual insights he offered into the nature of legal ordering was one that, unlike so much of that work, has failed to attract a great deal of attention. It concerned the way in which, under 'normal' conditions, citizens are in one important respect to be understood as alienated from the legal norms under which they live and are governed. That is, with respect to the existence of a valid legal system:

> the acceptance of the rules as common standards for the group may be split off from the relatively passive matter of the ordinary individual acquiescing in the rules by obeying them for his part alone ... The society in which this was so might be deplorably sheeplike; the sheep might end in the slaughter-house. But there is little reason for thinking that it could not exist or for denying it the title of a legal system.
>
> (Hart, 1961, p 114)

On the contrary: that is a legal system *working*.

Efforts to avoid or redress the legitimation of human suffering that happens in the name of the law, will be hampered by failing to see and understand that this too has been, and *is still*, a part of the potential and reality of law as a mode of organising social action. It is in this sense that a start-line attentiveness is required to the operation of the forces—including the structures and institutions of law—that maintain our distances from others, and that allow some to wreak havoc on the lives of others, and for this to be seen as normal and expected. These forces are many and they are no less powerful for being entirely commonplace. Yet insofar as legal norms are implicated amongst them, then the specificity of modern legal organisation—with its different roles, categories and compartmentalisations—and, just as importantly, as I have tried to show, its very particular intrigues with other social systems, together require an attentiveness to their social priority and their own 'dual use' in the face of the harms and suffering they sustain. Without this, practices of responsibility will all too readily continue to promote their other, with consequences that are all too depressingly predictable.

Bibliography

Agamben, G, *Homo Sacer: Sovereign Power and Bare Life*, 1998, Stanford, CA: Stanford University Press.

Agamben, G, *Remnants of Auschwitz: The Witness and the Archive*, 2002, Cambridge, MA: MIT Press.

Ahtisaari, M, *UN Security Council Report to the Secretary-General on Humanitarian Needs in Kuwait and Iraq in the Immediate Post-Crisis Environment by a Mission to the Area Led by Mr Martti Ahtisaari, Under-Secretary-General for Administration and Management*, 20 March 1991, annexed to a letter from the Secretary-General addressed to the President of the Security Council, UN Doc S/22366, accessed 2 January 2007, http://www.casi.org.uk/info/undocs/s22366.html.

Alexy, R, 'A defence of Radbruch's formula', in D Dyzenhaus (ed), *Recrafting the Rule of Law: the Limits of Legal Order*, 1999, Oxford: Hart, pp 15–39.

Alexy, R, 'The nature of legal philosophy', *Ratio Juris*, 2004, 17:2, pp 156–67.

Anghie, A, 'Finding the peripheries: sovereignty and colonialism in nineteenth-century international law', *Harvard International Law Journal*, 1999, 40:1, pp 1–80.

Arendt, H, *Eichmann in Jerusalem: A Report on the Banality of Evil*, 1977, Harmondsworth: Penguin.

Asad, T, 'On torture, or cruel, inhuman, and degrading treatment', *Social Research*, 1996, 63:4, pp 1081–109.

Bankowski, Z, *Living Lawfully: Love in Law and Law in Love*, 2001, Dordrecht: Kluwer.

Bartlett, R, '*Mabo*: another triumph for the common law', *Sydney Law Review*, 1993, 15:2, pp 178–86.

Bauman, Z, *Modernity and the Holocaust*, 1989, Cambridge: Polity.

Bauman, Z, *Society Under Siege*, 2002, Cambridge: Polity.

Beck, U, *Risk Society: Towards a New Modernity*, M Ritter (trans), 1992, London: Sage.

Beck, U, *Ecological Politics in an Age of Risk*, A Weisz (trans), 1995, Cambridge: Polity.

Bentham, J, *Truth versus Ashhurst*, 1792, accessed 30 July 2007, http://www.ucl.ac.uk/Bentham-Project/info/truthvash.htm.

Berger, J, 'The pain of living in the present world', *Le Monde Diplomatique* (English edn), February 2003, http://mondediplo.com/2003/02/15pain.

Berlin, I, 'Political ideas in the twentieth century', in *Four Essays on Liberty*, 1969, Oxford: Oxford University Press, pp 1–40.

Black, R, Henderson, H, Thomson, JM and Miller, K (eds), *The Laws of Scotland: Stair Memorial Encyclopaedia, Vol 11*, 1990, Edinburgh: Butterworths Law (Scotland).

Boughton & Ors (R on the application of) v HM Treasury [2006] EWCA Civ 504.

Bourdieu, P, 'The force of law: toward a sociology of the juridical field', *Hastings Law Journal*, 1987, 38:5, pp 814–53.

Bourke, J, *An Intimate History of Killing*, 2000, London: Granta.

Bovens, M, *The Quest for Responsibility: Accountability and Citizenship in Complex Organisations*, 1998, Cambridge: Cambridge University Press.

C v United Kingdom Application No 10358/83 (1983) 37 DR 142.

Calasso, R, *The Marriage of Cadmus and Harmony*, T Parks (trans), 1994, London: Vintage.

Campbell, D, Collins, H and Wightman, J (eds), *Implicit Dimensions of Contract*, 2003, Oxford: Hart.

Cane, P, *Responsibility in Law and Morality*, 2002, Oxford: Hart.

Christodoulidis, E and Veitch, S, 'The ignominy of unredeemed politics', *International Journal for Semiotics of Law*, 1997, X:29, pp 141–59.

Christodoulidis, E and Veitch, S (eds), *Lethe's Law: Justice, Law and Ethics in Reconciliation*, 2001, Oxford: Hart.

Cohen, S, *States of Denial: Knowing about Atrocities and Suffering*, 2001, Cambridge: Polity.

Coleman, J and Shapiro, S (eds), *The Oxford Handbook of Jurisprudence and Philosophy of Law*, 2002, Oxford: Oxford University Press.

Cover, R, '*Nomos* and narrative', 97 *Harvard Law Review*, 1983, pp 4–68.

Cover, R, 'Violence and the word', 95 *Yale Law Journal*, 1986, pp 1601–29.

Cubillo v Commonwealth [2000] FCA 1084.

Davis, M, *Late Victorian Holocausts: El Nino Famines and the Making of the Third World*, 2001, London: Verso.

Derrida, J, *The Gift of Death*, D Wills (trans), 1996, Chicago, IL: Chicago University Press.

Derrida, J, *On Cosmopolitanism and Forgiveness*, M Dooley and M Hughes (trans), 2001, London: Routledge.

Detmold, M, *The Unity of Law and Morality*, 1984, London: Routledge and Kegan Paul.

Douzinas, C, 'Humanity, military humanism and the new moral order', *Economy and Society*, 2003, 32:2, pp 159–83.

Dreyfus, HL and Rabinow, P (eds), *Michel Foucault: Beyond Structuralism and Hermeneutics*, 1983, Chicago, IL: University of Chicago Press.

Du Bois, F, ' "Nothing but the truth": the South African alternative to corrective justice in transitions to democracy', in E Christodoulidis and S Veitch (eds), *Lethe's Law: Justice, Law and Ethics in Reconciliation*, 2001, Oxford: Hart, pp 91–114.

Duff, A (ed), *Philosophy and the Criminal Law*, 1998, Cambridge: Cambridge University Press.

Dworkin, R, *Taking Rights Seriously*, 1977, London: Duckworth.

Dworkin, R, *Law's Empire*, 1986, London: Fontana.

Dworkin, R, *Sovereign Virtue: The Theory and Practice of Equality*, 2000, Cambridge, MA: Harvard University Press.

Dyzenhaus, D, *Judging the Judges, Judging Ourselves*, 1998, Oxford: Hart.

Dyzenhaus, D (ed), *Recrafting the Rule of Law: the Limits of Legal Order*, 1999, Oxford: Hart.

The Economist, 'Editorial: All wrong in Iraq', 8 April 2000, p 20.

Farmer, P, *Pathologies of Power: Health, Human Rights, and the New War on the Poor*, 2003, Berkeley, CA: University of California Press.

Fisk, R, *The Great War for Civilisation: The Conquest of the Middle East*, 2005, London: Fourth Estate.

Foucault, M, 'The subject and power', in HL Dreyfus and P Rabinow (eds), *Michel Foucault: Beyond Structuralism and Hermeneutics*, 1983, Chicago, IL: University of Chicago Press, pp 208–26.

Foucault, M, *The History of Sexuality Vol 1: An Introduction*, R Hurley (trans), 1990, London: Penguin.

Gaita, R, *A Common Humanity*, 1999, Melbourne: Text Publishing.

Galeano, E, *Upside Down: A Primer for the Looking Glass World*, M Fried (trans), 2000, New York: Picador.

Gardner, J, 'The mark of responsibility', *Oxford Journal of Legal Studies*, 2003, 23:2, pp 157–71.

Garland, D, 'The limits of the sovereign state', *British Journal of Criminology*, 1996, 36:4, pp 445–71.

Gazzini, T, *The Changing Rules on the Use of Force in International Law*, 2005, Manchester, Manchester University Press.

Giddens, A, 'Risk and responsibility', *Modern Law Review*, 1999, 62:1, pp 1–10.

Gilbert, K, *Living Black*, 1978, Harmondsworth: Penguin.

Gordon, J, 'When intent makes all the difference in the world: economic sanctions on Iraq and the accusation of genocide', 5 *Yale Human Rights and Development Law Journal*, 2002, pp 57–84.

Grass, G and Bourdieu, P, 'The "progressive" restoration: a Franco–German dialogue', 14 *New Left Review*, 2002, pp 63–77.

Habermas, J, *The Theory of Communicative Action Vol 2: Lifeworld and System*, T McCarthy (trans), 1987, Cambridge: Polity.

Habermas, J, *Between Facts and Norms*, W Rehg (trans), 1996, Cambridge, MA: MIT Press.

Habermas, J, 'Equal treatment of cultures and the limits of postmodern liberalism', *Journal of Political Philosophy*, 2005, 13:1, pp 1–28.

Hain, P, 'Comment: I fought apartheid, I'll fight Saddam', *The Guardian*, 6 January 2001, http://www.guardian.co.uk/Archive/Article/0,4273,4113256,00.html.

Harper, B, 'Letter to the editor', *Guardian Weekly*, 29 April 2004.

Hart, HLA, *The Concept of Law*, 1961, Oxford: Clarendon.

Hart, HLA, *Punishment and Responsibility*, 1968, Oxford: Clarendon.

Harvey, D, *The Condition of Postmodernity*, 1989, Oxford: Blackwell.

Hayek, F, *The Road to Serfdom*, 1944, London: Routledge.

Hindess, B, 'Fears of intrusion: antipolitical motifs in Western political discourse', in A Schedler (ed), *The End of Politics?*, 1997, Basingstoke: Macmillan, pp 21–39.

Hobbes, T, *Man and Citizen [De Homine et De Cive]*, B Gert (ed), 1991, Indianapolis, IN: Hackett.

Hobbes, T, *Leviathan*, R Tuck (ed), 1996, Cambridge: Cambridge University Press.

Horder, J (ed), *Oxford Essays in Jurisprudence* (Fourth Series), 2000, Oxford: Oxford University Press.

Human Rights and Equal Opportunity Commission, *Bringing Them Home: Report of the National Inquiry into the Forcible Removal of Aboriginal and Torres Strait Islander Children from their Families*, 1997, Sydney: HREOC.

Human Rights and Equal Opportunity Commission, *Social Justice Report*, 2005, Sydney: HREOC.

Hume, D, *A Treatise of Human Nature*, 2nd edn, 1978, Oxford: Oxford University Press.

Ireland, P, 'Recontractualising the corporation: implicit contract as ideology', in D Campbell, H Collins and J Wightman (eds), *Implicit Dimensions of Contract*, 2003, Oxford: Hart, pp 255–88.

James, W and Van de Vijver, L (eds), *After the TRC: Reflections on Truth and Reconciliation in South Africa*, 2000, Cape Town: David Philip.

Jonas, H, *The Imperative of Responsibility: In Search of an Ethics for the Technological Age*, 1984, Chicago, IL: University of Chicago Press.

Kamm, F, 'Rights', in J Coleman and S Shapiro (eds), *The Oxford Handbook of Jurisprudence and Philosophy of Law*, 2002, Oxford: Oxford University Press, pp 476–513.

Kampfner, J, 'Blood on his hands', *New Statesman*, 7 August 2006, accessed 6 January 2007, http://www.newstatesman.com/200608070017.

Kant, I, *The Metaphysics of Morals*, M Gregor (trans), 1991, Cambridge: Cambridge University Press.

Kelly, A, 'Introduction', in I Berlin, *Russian Thinkers*, 1979, Harmondsworth: Penguin.

Kerruish, V, 'Responding to *Kruger*: the constitutionality of genocide', 11 *Australian Feminist Law Journal*, 1998, pp 65–82.

Kerruish, V, 'Reconciliation, property and rights', in E Christodoulidis and S Veitch (eds), *Lethe's Law: Justice, Law and Ethics in Reconciliation*, 2001, Oxford: Hart, pp 191–205.

Kerruish, V and Perrin, C, 'Awash in colonialism', *Alternative Law Journal*, 1999, 24:1, pp 3–8.

Kerruish, V and Purdy, J, 'He "look honest": big white thief', *Law/Text/Culture*, 1998, 4:1, pp 146–71.

Koskenniemi, M, 'Faith, identity, and the killing of the innocent: international lawyers and nuclear weapons', 10 *Leiden Journal of International Law*, 1997, pp 137–62.

Koskenniemi, M, ' "The lady doth protest too much": Kosovo and the turn to ethics in international law', *Modern Law Review*, 2002, 65:2, pp 159–75.

Kruger v Commonwealth (1997) 146 ALR 126.

Kutz, C, 'Responsibility', in J Coleman and S Shapiro (eds), *The Oxford Handbook of Jurisprudence and Philosophy of Law*, 2002, Oxford: Oxford University Press, pp 458–87.

Lacey, N, ' "Philosophical foundations of the common law": social not metaphysical', in J Horder (ed), *Oxford Essays in Jurisprudence* (Fourth Series), 2000, Oxford: Oxford University Press, pp 17–39.

Lacey, N, 'Responsibility and modernity in criminal law', *Journal of Political Philosophy*, 2001, 9:3, pp 249–76.

Lamont, WD, *Law and the Moral Order*, 1981, Aberdeen: Aberdeen University Press.

Legality of the Threat or Use of Nuclear Weapons (Advisory Opinion) 1996, http://www.icj-cij.org.

Lieber, KA and Press, DG, 'The rise of US nuclear primacy', *Foreign Affairs*, 2006, 85:2, pp 42–54.

Lindqvist, S, *'Exterminate All the Brutes'*, 2002, London: Granta.

Lord Advocate's Reference No 1 of 2000, 2001, accessed 12 May 2007, http://www.scotcourts.gov.uk/opinions/11_00.html.

Loughlin, M, *Sword and Scales*, 2000, Oxford: Hart.

Loughlin, M, *The Idea of Public Law*, 2004, Oxford: Oxford University Press.

Lyotard, J-F, *The Differend: Phrases in Dispute*, G van den Abbeele (trans), 1988, Manchester: Manchester University Press.

Mabo v The State of Queensland (No 2) (1992) 175 CLR 1.

MacCormick, N, *Legal Reasoning and Legal Theory*, 1978, Oxford: Clarendon.

MacCormick, N, 'General legal concepts', in R Black, H Henderson, JM Thomson and K Miller (eds), *The Laws of Scotland: Stair Memorial Encyclopaedia, Vol 11*, 1990, Edinburgh: Butterworths Law (Scotland), pp 359–419.

MacCormick, N, 'Argumentation and interpretation in law', *Argumentation*, 1995, 9:3, pp 467–80.

MacCormick, N, *Rhetoric and the Rule of Law*, 2005, Oxford: Oxford University Press.

MacIntyre, A, *After Virtue: A Study in Moral Theory*, 2nd edn, 1985, London: Duckworth.

MacIntyre, A, *Whose Justice? Which Rationality?*, 1988, London: Duckworth.

Macwhirter, I, 'We're not Jock Tamson's bairns any more', *Sunday Herald*, 4 March 2007, http://www.sundayherald.com/oped/opinion/display.var.1234243.0.0.php?act +complaint&cid=116005.

Mamdani, M, 'A diminished truth', in W James and L Van de Vijver (eds), *After the TRC: Reflections on Truth and Reconciliation in South Africa*, 2000, Cape Town: David Philip, pp 32–41.

Mamdani, M, 'Amnesty or impunity? A preliminary critique of the *Report of the Truth and Reconciliation Commission of South Africa*', *Diacritics*, 2002, 32:3–4, pp 33–59.

Marx, K, 'On the Jewish question', in R Livingstone and G Barton (trans), *Marx: Early Writings*, 1975, Harmondsworth: Penguin, pp 211–41.

Marx, K, *Capital Vol 1*, 1990, London: Penguin.

Milgram, S, *Obedience to Authority*, 1974, New York: Harper and Row.

Mills, CW, *The Power Elite*, 1956, New York: Oxford University Press.

Milne, S, 'Britain: imperial nostalgia', *Le Monde Diplomatique* (English edn), May 2005, accessed 11 May 2007, http://mondediplo.com/2005/05/02empire.

Motha, S, 'Reconciliation as domination', in S Veitch (ed), *Law and the Politics of Reconciliation*, 2007, Aldershot: Ashgate, pp 69–93.

National Resources Defense Council, 'US nuclear forces: 2006', *Bulletin of Atomic Scientists*, 2006, 62:1, pp 68–71.

Nietzsche, F, *Beyond Good and Evil*, 1972, Harmondsworth: Penguin.

Nietzsche, F, *On the Genealogy of Morals*, 1996, Oxford: Oxford University Press.

Nino, C, *Radical Evil on Trial*, 1996, New Haven and London: Yale University Press.

Norrie, A, ' "Simulacra of morality"? Beyond the ideal/actual antinomies of criminal justice', in A Duff (ed), *Philosophy and the Criminal Law*, 1998, Cambridge: Cambridge University Press, pp 101–55.

Petersen, VC, 'The care *less* society and the erosion of individual responsibility', Paper presented to the Ethics in the New Millenium Conference, Ottawa, 24–28 September 2000, accessed 28 March 2007, http://strategis.ic.gc.ca/pics/oz/peterson.pdf.

Pilger, J, 'Iraq: paying the price', 2000, accessed 2 January 2007, http://www.johnpilger.com/page.asp?partid=11.

Pilger, J, *Freedom Next Time*, 2006, London: Bantam.

Pinter, H, 'Art, truth and politics', Nobel Lecture, 2005, accessed 5 January 2007, http://nobelprize.org/nobel_prizes/literature/laureates/2005/pinter-lecture.html.

Pogge, T, *World Poverty and Human Rights*, 2002, Cambridge: Polity.

Polanyi, K, *The Great Transformation: The Political and Economic Origins of Our Time*, 1957, Boston, MA: Beacon Press.

Power, M, 'From risk society to audit society', *Soziale Systeme*, 1997, 3:1, pp 3–21.

Power, S, '*A Problem from Hell': America and the Age of Genocide*, 2003, London: Flamingo.

Ricoeur, P, *The Just*, D Pellauer (trans), 2000, Chicago, IL: University of Chicago Press.

Rousseau, J-J, *The Social Contract and Discourses*, GDH Cole (trans), 1973, London: JM Dent.

Royal Commission on Aboriginal Deaths in Custody, *Final National Report*, 1991, Canberra: RCADC.

Salmond, J, *Jurisprudence*, 6th edn, 1920, London: Sweet and Maxwell.

Sands, P, *Lawless World*, 2006, London: Penguin.

Santos, B, *Toward a New Legal Common Sense*, 2002, London: Butterworths.

Schaap, A, 'Assuming responsibility in the hope of reconciliation', *Borderlands*, 2004, 3:1. accessed 21 March 2007, http://www.borderlandsejournal.adelaide.edu.au/vol3no1_2004/schaap_hope.htm.

Schall, JV, 'Justice: the most terrible of the virtues', *Journal of Markets and Morality*, 2004, 7:2, pp 409–21.

Schedler, A (ed), *The End of Politics?*, 1997, Basingstoke: Macmillan.

Schell, J, *The Fate of the Earth*, 1982, London: Jonathan Cape.

Simons, G, *The Scourging of Iraq: Sanctions, Law and Natural Justice*, 2nd edn, 1998, London: Macmillan.

Smith, A, *An Inquiry into the Nature and Causes of the Wealth of Nations,* RH Campbell and AS Skinner (eds), 1976, Oxford: Oxford University Press.

Smith, A, 'Early draft of part of *The Wealth of Nations*', in A Smith, *Lectures on Jurisprudence*, RL Meek, DD Raphael and PG Stein (eds), 1978, Oxford: Oxford University Press, pp 562–81.

Smith, S, 'How law hides risk', in G Teubner, L Farmer and D Murphy (eds), *Environmental Law and Ecological Responsibility*, 1994, Chichester: John Wiley and Sons, pp 117–44.

South African Truth and Reconciliation Commission, *Truth and Reconciliation Commission of South Africa Report*, 1998, Cape Town: Juta.

Southern Rhodesia, In re [1919] AC 211.

Stapleton, J, 'Perspectives on causation', in J Horder (ed), *Oxford Essays in Jurisprudence* (Fourth Series), 2000, Oxford: Oxford University Press, pp 61–84.

Strawson, J (ed), *Law after Ground Zero*, 2002, London: Glasshouse.

Summers, RS, 'Two types of substantive reason: the core of a theory of common-law justification', *Cornell Law Review*, 1978, 63:5, pp 707–88.

Tadros, V, *Criminal Responsibility*, 2005, Oxford: Oxford University Press.

Teubner, G, Farmer, L and Murphy, D (eds), *Environmental Law and Ecological Responsibility*, 1994, Chichester: John Wiley and Sons.

Tully, J, 'The unfreedom of the moderns in comparison to their ideals of constitutional democracy', *Modern Law Review*, 2002, 65:2, pp 204–28.

Ullmann-Margalit, E, 'Invisible-hand explanations', *Synthese*, 1978, 39:20, pp 263–91.

Unger, RM, *False Necessity: Anti-Necessitarian Social Theory in the Service of Radical Democracy*, 1987, Cambridge: Cambridge University Press.

United Kingdom Parliament's Select Committee on International Development, 'Second Report on the Impact of Sanctions', 2000, accessed 2 January 2007, http://www.publications.parliament.uk/pa/cm199900/cmselect/cmintdev/67/6707.htm.

United Nations Children's Fund, 'Iraq donor update', 11 July 2001, accessed 5 July 2006, http://www.casi.org.uk/info/un.html#unicef.

United Nations Children's Fund Information Newsline, 'Iraq surveys show "humanitarian emergency"', 12 August 1999, accessed 2 January 2007, http://www.unicef.org/newsline/99pr29.htm.

United Nations Security Council Panel on Humanitarian Issues, *Report of the Second Panel Established Pursuant to the Note by the President of the Security Council of 30 January 1999 (S/1999/100), Concerning the Current Humanitarian Situation in Iraq*, 1999, accessed 2 January 2007, http://www.casi.org.uk/info/panelrep.html.

United States Nuclear Posture Review, *Nuclear Posture Review Report*, submitted to Congress 31 December 2001, excerpts accessed 12 May 2007, http://www.globalsecurity.org/wmd/library/policy/dod/npr.htm.

Veitch, S (ed), *Law and the Politics of Reconciliation*, 2007, Aldershot: Ashgate.

Watson, I, 'Buried alive', *Law and Critique*, 2002, 13:3, pp 253–69.

Weber, M, 'Bureaucracy', in *Economy and Society, Vol 2*, G Roth and C Wittich (eds), 1978, Berkeley, CA: University of California Press, pp 956–1005.

Williams, AT, 'Human rights and law: between sufferance and insufferability', 123 *Law Quarterly Review*, 2007, pp 133–58.

Williams, RA, *The American Indian in Western Legal Thought: Discourses of Conquest*, 1990, Oxford: Oxford University Press.

Woodward, W, 'Nuclear deterrent not the solution, says Clarke', *The Guardian*, 26 September 2006, p 9.

World Bank, *World Development Report: Attacking Poverty*, 2000–01, synopsis accessed 3 April 2007, www.worldbank.org.

World Health Organization, 'Health situation in Iraq', 26 February 2001, Brussels, accessed 2 January 2007, http://www.humanitarianinfo.org/sanctions/handbook/docs_handbook/who-kreisel6386.pdf.

Yorta Yorta Aboriginal Community v Victoria (Yorta Yorta) [2002] HCA 58.

Young, E, 'Aboriginal health lagging 100 years behind', *New Scientist*, 30 April 2007, http://www.newscientist.com/article.ns?id=dn11747.

Zimbardo, P, *The Lucifer Effect: How Good People Turn Evil*, 2007, London: Rider.

Zizek, S, *Did Somebody Say Totalitarianism?*, 2001a, London: Verso.

Zizek, S, 'What can Lenin tell us about freedom today?', *Rethinking Marxism*, 2001b, 13:2, pp 1–9.

Index

CPSIA information can be obtained
at www.ICGtesting.com
Printed in the USA
FFOW03n0815120117
31219FF